W9-CLZ-361

The Bones of the Earth

Books by Howard Mansfield

Cosmopolis

In the Memory House

Skylark

The Same Ax, Twice

The
Bones *of the*
Earth

DISCARD

Howard
Mansfield

Shoemaker S&H Hoard *Washington, D.C.*

Library of Congress Cataloging-in-Publication Data
Mansfield, Howard.
The bones of the earth / Howard Mansfield.
p. cm.
ISBN 1–59376–040-X
Includes bibliographical references.
1. Mansfield, Howard. 2. Historic sites—New Hampshire.
3. Natural history—New Hampshire. 4. New Hampshire—
Social life and customs. 5. New Hampshire—History, Local.
6. New Hampshire—Biography. 7. Hancock (N.H.)—
Biography. I. Title.
F40.M36 2004
974.2'043'092—dc22   2004011661

Text design by David Bullen
Printed in the United States of America

Shoemaker 〔S̲H̲〕 Hoard
A Division of Avalon Publishing Group Inc.
Distributed by Publishers Group West

10 9 8 7 6 5 4 3 2 1

Once again, and always,
for Dr. B. A. Millmoss

Contents

The Bones | *of the* Earth

Introduction

Starting from Paumanok

When I grew up, the view from my backyard was Long Island's story told in one farm. A fertile corn field stood awaiting the bulldozer. This farm was bordered by the woods we all played in—hide and seek, army, and looking for box turtles. We were baby boomers living in a "development." We watched the rest of the boom: fields of cabbages, corn, potatoes gone in the wink of an eye to houses, stores, and new schools. I remember these smells: fields of raw, bulldozed mud—thick-clay muck that trapped your sneakers—freshly-sawn lumber, and the new paint in the just-opened schools. To this day I associate drying paint with the optimism of beginnings.

That farm behind my house went for someone else's fresh start, for their American Dream. But after it was gone I felt that the world was less open. My father put up a fence for the first time. Now when I visit, the small yard is hemmed in by a showroom of fence styles: chain link, split rail, stockade. In the old photos there is the horizon; acres of corn and woods, a barn in the far distance, and all that fabulous Long Island light spilling in.

One farm, one backyard—this, in short, formed the central questions that I explore as a writer: What makes an American place? Why are we using the world's greatest wealth to create ugliness? Is America still "a poem in our eyes," as Ralph Waldo Emerson wrote?

All these questions examine the notion of "sense of place," a phrase that has entered advertising and been eroded by over-use. My last few books have examined place in New England. *In the Memory House* looks at the stories we tell ourselves as a culture, the ways we choose our ancestors. *The Same Ax, Twice: Restoration and Renewal in a Throwaway Age* examines how we can live with the past in ways that will save the future.

I live and write in New Hampshire, where in the manner of all journeys—sideways, by chance—my wife and I arrived twenty years ago. We live in a small town (Hancock, population 1,700) on eight acres of old pasture and forest bordering on a brook. We keep a small flock of chickens in the barn, and one black-and-white pig, Christopher Hogwood, who lives a royal life. (He was a runt who would have been dispatched with the back end of a shovel if we had not taken him in. He arrived as a sickly thing in a shoe box. Today, more than a dozen years later, he weighs 750 pounds and commands an empire of slops and visitors. The last shall be first.)

My wife, Sy Montgomery, travels the world to write about vanishing wildlife. She has written *Walking with the Great Apes, Spell of the Tiger, Journey of the Pink Dolphins,* and *Search for the Golden Moon Bear.* She has put in hard travels in Africa, Borneo, India, the Amazon, Laos, and Cambodia, where she has seen, over and over, the fall of the wild and the agrarian for this new world we are building in great haste. Basically, the story of one farm, one forest, acre by acre, turned under for someone's dream, and the world is less open.

❦

"How'd you come to live up there?" I am asked on occasion, "You're a flatlander." I grew up on the flattest land there is on the East Coast, I answer. The highest point on Long Island is in my hometown of Huntington, Jayne's Hill, which is all of 400 feet above sea level. Just downhill, Walt Whitman was born, and from here the child set forth to wander "fish-shape Paumanok," an ancient Indian name for the island that Whitman used in his poems.

"My infancy, childhood, youth and manhood were all pass'd on Long Island, which I sometimes feel as if I had incorporated," Whitman wrote in his short memoir. "I roam'd, as boy and man, and have lived in nearly all parts, from Brooklyn to Montauk point. . . . As I write, the whole experience comes back to me after the lapse of forty and more years—the soothing rustle of the waves, and the saline smell—boyhood's times, the clam-digging, barefoot, and with trowsers roll'd up—hauling down the creek—the perfume of the sedge-meadows —the hay-boat, and the chowder and fishing excursions. . . ."

No one read Whitman much when I was growing up, but they would put his name on things like a high school, or the flag of the *Long-Islander,* the town weekly he founded. In 1962 they put his name on a mall. The Walt Whitman Mall. In that name is one part of the American journey, from a boisterous individualism to a lock-step consumerism. (Out of the cradle endlessly shopping.)

The Walt Whitman Mall was the first enclosed mall on Long Island. An enclosed mall was such a new thing that the developers disguised the inside to be as much like the outside as possible. Small goldfish ponds along the way were crossed by short bridges as in a Japanese Garden, and there were two large cages of singing birds. I suppose the developers were concerned that people would be uncomfortable inside, or maybe they were unknowingly making a small offering of amends to the spirits of the place they had just paved over. The mall was built on a farm that had grown vegetables for the Chinese restaurants in New York. There had been grand old oaks, which Whitman had known in his boyhood. The oaks, of course, were cut down.

In the go-go, greed-is-good 1980s, the interior of the mall was remodeled. Out went the goldfish, the greenery, and the bird song. The new look was sleek white metal and mirrors. The architect probably called it "high-tech." People were used to being indoors by then; summer meant air-conditioning. When the mall was first built, if you were hot in your car, you rolled down the window; if you were hot at home, you opened the windows and turned on a fan; or you sat outside, often with the neighbors and a few cold beers. One or two families had pools—round, metal, four- or five-foot deep above-ground pools—and they likely regretted it, as they were soon invaded by every kid in the neighborhood. The August heat on Long Island could settle in, a humid, unmoving mass of air that seemed to press down on you like a big hand.

Whitman's birthplace is right across the road from his mall—across a large parking lot, and four lanes of Route 110. His small house is wedged between a mini-mall and a furniture store. About the time the mall was built there was a big debate about moving his birthplace. The Whitman house was to be moved to a historic park, a subdivision of other displaced historic houses. This is an idea that makes sense only if you have lived in a land newly sprung from the zoning code—in the ideal code-world, houses and stores, history and the present, the old and the young never touch or mix. Everything is in its zone, and you drive from zone to zone. Whitman stayed put; wiser heads prevailed by pointing out that you can't move a birthplace.

We went to the new mall when it opened, and for years after, it was the place you went to buy birthday presents or gifts for the holidays. The name of the mall never sat right with me; it never achieved the invisibility of the common place. I would puzzle over it—the Walt Whitman Mall—what would Whitman think? At the time of the first Earth Day, I knew Whitman only as a poet of nature. But there are many Whitmans ("I contain multitudes")—the Whitman of lilacs in the dooryard and his boyhood "isle of sweet brooks of drinking water," the Whitman who celebrated crossing Brooklyn Ferry, and the Whitman who loved to ride with teamsters in the Broadway crowds. There's the jingoistic Whitman with his patriotic yawps, the nurse Whitman to the Civil War wounded, and the gay Whitman of the Calamus love poems.

What would Walt Whitman think of his mall? I now think that he might like to hang out on some days, a big, bearded man, looking like the homeless or the aimless of our city streets and parks. The mall security force would keep an eye on him, buzzing past him, suggesting that he move along now.

These days when I think of Walt Whitman at the Walt Whitman Mall, I see him sitting in the back of a powder-blue mall security car. The two-way radio is squawking up front as the rent-a-cop fills out some official report. Whitman turns and looks out with a grand grin.

☯

From the many Whitmans I take away many lessons: to sing of the crowd and of solitude, of the open road and the old towns and forests along the way. To look at them squarely and save the polemics for the think-tank boys and girls on the conference circuit. (Well, okay, that last sentence is polemical. As Whitman wrote, "Do I contradict myself? Very well then I contradict myself.") From Whitman, my hometown neighbor, I take these lines as guidance:

> *From Paumanok starting I fly like a bird,*
> *Around and around to soar to sing the idea of all,*
> *To the north betaking myself to sing there arctic songs,*
> *To Kanada till I absorb Kanada in myself, to Michigan then,*
> *To Wisconsin, Iowa, Minnesota, to sing their songs, (they are*
> *   inimitable;)*
> *Then to Ohio and Indiana to sing theirs, to Missouri and*
> *   Kansas and Arkansas to sing theirs. . . .*

☯

That is the outlook, but in this book we stay close to the ground. This is a book about landmarks, but of the oldest kind—sticks and stones. For millennia this is all there was: sticks and stones, dirt and trees, animals and people, the sky by day and night. This was the world's order by day and by night in dreams. The Lord spoke through burning bushes and rocks, through lightning and oaks. Trees and rocks and water were holy. They are commodities today, and that is part of our disquiet.

Part I, Axis Mundi, is about finding the center, marking the land and time, to join the temporal and eternal, earth and heaven. Part II, Flaneurs, is about learning to be tourists of the near-at-hand, looking close to home at changes in the land. Part III, Rpm, is about the force that topples the old axis mundi, unsettling us and the land.

That's it: time and change in the land. Sticks and stones and how they dance in our dreams.

"In these studies I have sought to re-name the things seen, now lost in the chaos of borrowed titles, many of them inappropriate, under which the true character lies hid," William Carlos Williams introduced *In the American Grain*. I would amend the great poet: I have sought to *un*name "the things seen" and remind us of the things unseen.

෧෨

And lastly, a dedication. These pages are for the tourist who entered the Hancock Cash Market a few years ago. The market is our general store in the center of Main Street. Pat Higgins was then in the pivotal role of cashier, which is like being the mayor of Main Street. (The job requires dispensing the news of births and illnesses, giving directions to lost delivery men, holding packages for residents, running a lost-and-found, and keeping track— the general who-just-went-up-the-street news.)

"Do you have Vermont maple syrup?" the tourist asked Pat.

Pat pointed to the shelves of maple syrup made in town and said, "We have New Hampshire maple syrup."

"Don't you have *Vermont* maple syrup?" he persisted.

"Don't you know where you are?" Pat asked him.

That's exactly the question. Let us be like Whitman. Starting from wherever you are now, fly and sing the song of your place. (And for God's sake, New Hampshire is not Vermont— and the residents of both states are relieved.)

I | Axis Mundi

The Walking
Stick & | the Edge
of the Universe

Boston Post Cane

In pre-Christian times, some small villages were gathered around a roland, a post or sacred tree that marked the center of the world. All the world moved around that axis. The Christians took over the old pagan symbols; the sacred tree became the cross. Today we live in a world of many centers and still long for an *axis mundi,* a marked center of our known world. (Hence all the talk of community and "sense of place" and "social capital.")

Walking staffs were symbols of the axis mundi. In New England a historic walking staff is having a small revival. This walking stick was a promotional gimmick for a newspaper. That newspaper is dead, and the gimmick is now an honorable tradition.

Edwin Grozier bought the nearly-bankrupt *Boston Post* in 1891, determined to make it the "great breakfast table paper of New

England." In two-and-a-half years, Grozier increased the *Boston Post*'s circulation from 30,000 to more than 100,000 with a series of promotions and contests.

He promised to give away "a Ford a day" to the reader sending in the best news item. He convinced 60,000 children to send in their pennies to help the *Post* buy three elephants for the Franklin Park Zoo (Mollie, Waddy, and Tony). He had his photographers troll New England with a movie scout looking for pretty young women. (Circulation increased by 10,000 copies the first week.) The *Post* also printed photos of "headless women." If a woman identified herself she could show up at the newspaper in the same clothes to claim ten dollars in gold. Grozier made another play for the readership of women when, in a "daring experiment," he published an all-women-edited Sunday edition in 1894. The special edition sold over 100,000 copies.

But Grozier's most successful stunt was the *Boston Post* Cane. He sent letters to selectmen in Massachusetts, Rhode Island, Maine, and New Hampshire offering them a cane that they could present to the town's oldest male citizen. The cane was made of African ebony with an engraved gold-plated head. Grozier asked the selectmen to return a form telling the newspaper about the town's oldest resident; to what did he credit his long life? "They will present an interesting galaxy of the vigor and longevity of New England manhood," said the *Post*.

The cane was a hit. There were more ceremonies and celebrations than the *Post* could cover. "The towns made this what it is. It's a uniting talisman that meant a lot to them," said Lincoln Charles, who has researched making reproduction canes at his company, Charles Non-Ferrous Castings. "The cane is more important than his newspaper ever was. The cane is important because people supported it with their feelings." The cane represents a hunger for ancient order; to mark one spot as the axis, the center of the earth, and say this much is certain.

In the 1930s, Edwin Grozier's son, Richard, who had taken over the paper after his father's death, allowed as how women were worthy to receive the cane. They had won the vote in 1920; they were ready to hold the *Boston Post* Cane.

The *Boston Post* folded in 1956, that high year of suburban exodus and downtown decline. But the cane lives. Towns keep passing it along to their elders. By and by some canes were lost; some towns dropped the practice. You can see how it happened. After someone dies, it is awkward to come calling on the family for the cane. (Imagine the discussion among the selectmen: "You go; no *you* go.") Some canes are in attics, some canes were buried with the honorees, and some families reportedly refused to return the cane (even though the gold head is engraved "to be transmitted"). The cane originally given to Vassalboro, Maine, was found in the 1980s at a yard sale in California. A resident of Leominister, Massachusetts, bought back his town's cane for $595 at a Maine auction. And the Lee, Massachusetts, cane was rescued from the rubbish heap at a Masonic home for the elderly.

Eleanor Burns spent two years searching for the canes in the 1980s. Four of her relatives have received a cane. Burns figures that the *Post* handed out 431 canes in 1909. (Others say there were 700 canes.) She could account for 400 canes: 182 were held by women; 74 by men; and 112 were kept by a town or historical society. Twenty-seven towns had lost their canes; three were destroyed in fires; and two were held by people who were not the town's oldest, but refused to give them up.

Today some towns are reviving the tradition, having replicas built, or looking around for the original. Some towns keep the cane in a glass case and award a certificate. The cane is a way to tether a town to time and place. We are so mobile these days and live such separate lives that it's almost as if we hover over the earth.

In Epping, New Hampshire, the cane was lost more than fifty years ago. The last recipient was Jacob Milter Blye who died at the age of ninety-eight in 1944. Epping has ordered two replacements (at $265 a cane), one for display and one to hand out. Peterborough, New Hampshire, has also resumed honoring its eldest citizen with a replica cane.

Dennis, Massachusetts, began awarding the cane again in

2000, after stopping in 1977. The cane was given to 107-year-old Elizabeth Smith (who, her daughter said, was as "healthy as a horse. She hasn't seen a doctor in fifty years. She hasn't taken an aspirin in . . . I don't remember when.")

In Greenville, New Hampshire, the cane was "anonymously returned" in 1993 after it had been missing for several years. The cane was repaired and awarded that year to Clara Caron, 98. She was born in 1895, the oldest of five girls. When her mother died, her father left the girls in a Worcester, Massachusetts, orphanage for three years. He remarried and reunited his family. Looking for work, he sent Clara by train to see if the Greenville mills were hiring. They were, and the family followed. Clara was paid thirteen dollars for a fifty-four-hour week, she recalled, which was good pay then. She gave her wages to her father in an unopened envelope; he gave her fifty cents a week to spend. The cane can act as an axis mundi, recalling the ancient center, the old order.

In Hampton, New Hampshire, the cane had been retired to the vault at the town offices in 1973 or 1974. "People started to fear getting the cane," said Town Clerk Jane Kelley. "The cane would be given out, and within a week, that person would be dead. It was awful."

People in many towns saw the cane as the scythe of the grim reaper, the ultimate send-off gift. It was like being voted next-to-die. Three New Hampshire towns lost their oldest residents on the same day, November 14, 2001: Lillian Werner, 99, of Chester; Nellie Bassett, 99, of Fremont; and Alice M. Savage, 103, of Henniker. (In Stephen King's *Needful Things,* Aunt Evvie died at age 91, two years after receiving the cane.)

The selectmen in Hampton also began to fear the cane. They were no longer certain who was the oldest person in town. "We were having problems with people in nursing homes, and there was no way to find out who was the oldest or was a native," said Selectman Ashton Norton. "Then we'd give the cane out, and we'd get complaints that we didn't give it to the right person. It got to be so much trouble that the board decided to leave it in the town office building."

Fremont, New Hampshire, was also having trouble identifying its oldest citizens. "We've had a complete turnover of true natives versus newcomers. The *Boston Post* Cane holders will go to people in town twenty years or under before you know it," said local historian Matthew Thomas. You "don't know if the oldest in town is your next door neighbor," he said.

Awarding the cane to the oldest native resident does restore the axis mundi. Here, for a moment, attention is paid to someone's entire lifetime. They are honored for surviving, for just being there, certainly, but the community can see the shape of that life: the honor of work and sacrifice, the tragedies of lost children and spouses, and the pride in great-grandchildren.

But many times it is difficult to find this true center. The oldest resident is not in residence. She or he has been removed to a nursing home. The *Boston Post* Cane shows us the true arrangement of our lives: our villages are not gathered around the oldest tree. We don't live in a hierarchy from old to young. The cane accidentally maps the new territory—the village without its roland, the world of many centers.

This is why the cane was set aside in many places. The old might be miles away in a nursing home. Or if a nursing home is in town, some "nonresidents"—born elsewhere, come here to die—can claim a long tenure.

Who deserves the honor? In some old-age homes it is not unusual for a half-dozen centenarians to sit together at dinner. (Elizabeth Smith, the 107-year-old cane holder from Dennis, had six other people at her birthday party who were over 100 years old, including another cane-holder who was 108.) Seven hundred years of life at one table. We have not yet adjusted to a world in which 700 years of human experience can break bread together.

Edwin Grozier had in mind the tall tales told by the hot-stove in the village general store. "A man who has cheated death is always an interesting figure," he said. He had an old newspaperman's love of the "most"—beautiful, tragic, unusual. . . . He thought of the cane so he could print stories that asked: To what do you owe your longevity? Answer: Hard work, a teaspoon of vinegar in the morning and of whiskey at night. That sort of thing. Never saw a doctor in ninety-eight years. Saw the Red Sox win the series once in 1918; not leaving 'till they win the series again. Lived here your whole life? Not yet. A staple of old newspapering.

The *Post* published these stories as "a tribute to honored and useful lives, to thrift, temperance, and right living." The first cane holders ascribed their longevity to "total abstinence from intoxicating liquors and tobacco" and "industry and sobriety" and "moderation in all things." Except for the spirited Stillman Parkhurst of Bedford, New Hampshire, who said he had "never lain in the gutter much" and Richard Currier of Deerfield, New Hampshire, who reported that he was "drunk throughout his life."

The elderly still have much to tell us. But that question about longevity? We welcome the homespun answer, but know the answer is in part: good genes, a hip operation, these pills and that CAT Scan, and miles of paperwork for all the Medicare and health insurance.

If the *Boston Post* Cane is in a glass case in town hall, then so too is aging, shut away in a nursing home, and so too is dying, with its complicated questions about when to end treatment, when to unplug, how to ease pain and let go. If the cane is buried in the town safe, then it is representative of our fear of death. In the old order, life and death held hands in the village center.

Radio Telescope

The *Boston Post* Cane marks time in increments we can understand: one life, one generation at a time. It has only been eleven generations since the founding of America, one hundred generations since Christ, people say. We picture the generations, each as one representative person, holding hands across the years, as if lined up in a field. In this way, we see our lives on the axis of time.

In my town, Hancock, New Hampshire, and nine other

towns across the country, there is a new axis mundi, a radio telescope, part of the Very Long Baseline Array. The radio telescope moves to the time of the cosmos.

It's a big white dish—one hundred feet tall, eighty-two feet wide—far bigger than anything else around here. The nearest small city is about twenty miles away, and even it doesn't have a ten-story building. This big dish is in the woods, a white saucer against the green. From the top of Skatutakee mountain, you can see the dish moving, pursuing its private thoughts, an attentive cat's ear thrown back, listening.

The New Hampshire dish moves in concert with the other nine to create a single 5,000-mile-wide radio telescope, making it the world's largest astronomical instrument. The VLBA —the inevitable big-science, big-project letter pile-up—has been operating since 1993. The National Radio Astronomy Observatory has its big white dishes from St. Croix in the Virgin Islands to Mauna Kea, Hawaii, with stops in between for North Liberty, Iowa; Los Alamos and Pie Town, New Mexico; Fort Davis, Texas; Kitts Peak, Arizona; Owens Valley, California; Brewster, Washington, and our dish here in Hancock.

We have the hardware, a 240-ton piece of the chase. It's straightforward—the dish resting on its huge "bull gear" gathers the signal and focuses it down several tubes—a reverse gramophone horn—where the noise is frozen—cooled with helium gas close to absolute zero—to reveal the "true signal." This signal is amplified and recorded on miles of tape—about three miles to a reel. Each day, the two technicians who manage the Hancock dish ship a reel or two of tape by Fed-Ex to the New Mexico center. Out of the ancient noise, scientists create images of the universe—abstract art in egg-yolk yellow, deep purple, and azure.

The radio telescopes are seeking out black holes, quasars, protostars, and the outside curve of the Milky Way galaxy. There are many mysteries; a strange gamma ray burst from someplace 7 billion light years away; the magnetic field on the surface of a star a mere 1000 light years away. In 1995 scientists at the national radio observatory reported finding what may be the biggest black hole known—about 90,000 light years across —with a mass equal to 40 million suns. The black hole is in the center of a galaxy 21 million light years away. It's rotating at up to 650 miles a second. These are Alice-in-Wonderland numbers—40 million suns, 21 million light years, 650 miles a second. We take the astronomers at their word (that there is even something called a light year) because we think in lifetimes; we lean on the *Boston Post* Cane for our perception of time.

These discoveries flash across our daily news, and they are reported and forgotten before anyone has to admit that we really don't comprehend what any of this means—except that it is strange, far away, and involves a kind of time that has nothing to do with us, no matter what physicists have been saying for a hundred years.

Intent on proving its worth to doubting taxpayers, the National Radio Astronomy Observatory produces some alarming press releases. "Ancient Black Hole Speeds Through Sun's Galactic Neighborhood, Devouring Companion Star" was the headline of an announcement in 2001. "Neighborhood" is a diminutive setting for this thug star. The roller coaster-like path in the illustration—"Black Hole's Wild Ride Through the Milky Way"—made me woozy. And I was once, in my youth, a backyard astronomer and a member in good standing of the Long Island Observers Association.

Astronomers these days are looking back in time twelve billion years. The universe is thought to have begun fourteen billion years ago with the "big bang." They are viewing objects that are nearly at the edge of the observable universe, bringing us the news of creation. This modern axis mundi is like the first roland, a tree of life, joining earth and heavens.

The
Washington | Elm
Reassembled

Ulmus cincinnatus

Watson Grant Cutter was six years old in 1844. He had a firm
memory of that year, the year his mother died. Every Sunday
his family would visit relatives around Cambridge. His family
went back a long way in town. Four of his great-grandfathers
had fought in the Revolution. One of them was present when
Washington took command of the Continental Army in Cambridge. This, too, was a firm memory, a story told in each
generation.

Each Sunday, in the horse-drawn carriage, they would ride
beneath the Washington Elm, which stood in the middle of
Garden Street. "At that time the Washington Elm was a magnificent tree; it was not the tallest tree in the neighborhood,
but it was the most spreading. Its branches covered the entire
street from fence to fence and it was impossible to drive
through the street without passing under it. As we passed

under it my father and my mother would say, 'Children, this is the Washington Elm; under it Washington took command of the army in 1775. Always remember it. We were told so by our parents and they were told so by their fathers, who were here at the time. This is historic ground,'" Cutter told the Cambridge chapter of the Sons of the American Revolution in 1907. Cutter was vice president of the chapter.

"Gentlemen," he addressed the meeting, "to our ancestors that tree and that ground were not only historic, they were sacred, and should be the same to us and our descendants." Cutter had lost his mother early in life, but he could find solace in a large family. Watson Grant Cutter believed in his ancestors; he believed in George Washington and the Washington Elm. He did not worship alone.

"*July 3d.* — General Washington is here," Dorothy Dudley wrote in her diary. "His appearance is one to inspire confidence and love, and to make us grateful for the possession of such a chief. To-day he formally took command, under one of the grand old elms on the Common. It was a magnificent sight. The majestic figure of the General, mounted on his horse beneath the wide-spreading branches of the patriarch tree; the multitude thronging the plain around, and the houses filled with interested spectators of the scene, while the air rung with shouts of enthusiastic welcome, as he drew his sword, and thus declared himself Commander-in-chief of the Continental army."

The Washington Elm was a sacred witness to the birth of the nation. "This tree is our most precious relic," said the Hannah Winthrop Chapter of the Daughters of the American Revolution in their 1907 guide to historic Cambridge. A photo of the elm faces the title page. "As a shrine of the Revolution, a temple 'not made with hands,' and the only living witness of the scenes of a hundred years ago, we trust the old elm will long survive, a sacred memorial to those who shall come after us," said the program of Cambridge's centennial observance of the Revolution in 1875.

Each story about the elm uses the same words: historic,

　　　　　　　　　　　　　　　HOWARD MANSFIELD

sacred, hallowed, witness. Many believed the elm was a survivor of the forest primeval, "a guardian genius of the place." "May no unkind hand mar the last tree of the native forest," said the *American Magazine* in 1837. "Glorious old tree, that has stood in sight of the smoke of Lexington and Bunker's Hill battles, and weathered the storms of many generations,—worthy of reverence." The Washington Elm had grown with the young nation.

The elm was a site of pilgrimage. "Visitors from all lands come with interest to the spot, gaze into the spreading branches, and account themselves happy if they can bear away a twig as a sacred token," reported the *Atlantic Monthly* in 1875. These sacred tokens traveled far. The wood from a fallen limb was made into a chair exhibited at the Centennial Exposition in Philadelphia. Many historical societies have a piece of the Washington Elm in a glass case. There are enough pieces in different museums—twigs and chunks of fallen limbs—that if you were to gather them, it seems that you could reassemble the Washington Elm. I imagine the elm reassembled like a dinosaur skeleton, the reconstructed tree standing in a big white exhibition hall, the real wood wired with the conjectural. (But if the reassembly was as speculative as some dinosaur exhibits, the roots would be in the air, the crown underground, and the trunk taking off who knows where.)

The Washington Elm appeared on postcards, stereoscope slides, china, upholstery, a one-cent stamp, the Cambridge city seal, in histories by Washington Irving and Senator Henry Cabot Lodge, and schoolbooks like the *Young Folks' Life of Washington*. The tree was doted upon and scrutinized by botanists. The trunk circumference, three feet above the ground, measured twelve feet, two-and-a-half inches in 1844, and forty years later just a little more, fourteen feet, one inch. It was one hundred feet tall, with a spreading crown of about ninety feet, and had about seven million leaves, calculated one Harvard professor.

Distinguished visitors, like the Prince of Wales, were taken to see the tree. Harvard's president had arranged that visit in 1860. He "had made up his mind that a very spectacular event in the Prince's visit would be the introduction of George Washington under the Washington Elm to the Prince of Wales," recalled a bystander. George Washington, a descendant of Washington's youngest brother, was in Harvard's Class of 1864. "He was a tall, raw-boned youth, with slightly reddish brown hair, blue eyes, corresponding pretty closely to what the mighty Washington himself might have looked like. . . . The carriage of the Prince of Wales and the Duke of Newcastle stopped at the Washington Elm, the meaning of which I do not imagine the Prince understood or cared about, and poor George Washington was led up to be introduced to him." Neither man was pleased. (Washington, a Confederate soldier, was killed in the Civil War.)

The venerated tree was accorded more honors as it aged. In 1847 a reverend encircled the elm with a cast iron fence to protect it from traffic. In 1864 Cambridge planted a granite slab in front of the tree with an inscription said to have been written by Henry Wadsworth Longfellow:

> UNDER THIS TREE
> WASHINGTON
> FIRST TOOK COMMAND
> OF THE
> AMERICAN ARMY
> JULY 3D, 1775

For the centennial of the Revolution, the tree was dressed up, with flags like ribbons in its hair. An American flag flew above the tree's crown from a pole attached to the trunk, and smaller flags hung from the lower limbs, "covering it with a perfect glory of stars and stripes," said the official record of the celebration. A life-sized portrait of Washington on horseback was placed in front of the tree. A few paces from the elm, a decorated arch was erected in the street so it framed the painting. The top of the arch said, "Birthplace of the American Army," and the pillars bore the dates 1775 and 1875, each date honored with a laurel. A little above this were painted swags of flowers. The arch was bordered with stars and topped with a large eagle and two more American flags. The ceremony began with a procession that passed under the arch on its way to hear the day's speeches and James Russell Lowell's ode, "Under the Old Elm."

"Historic town, thou holdest sacred dust," Lowell said in the opening stanza, noting Cambridge's reputation as "pious, learned, just."

> But Memory greets with reverential kiss
> No spot in all thy circuit as sweet as this,
> Touched by that modest glory as it past,
> O'er which yon elm hath piously displayed
> These hundred years its monumental shade.

The monuments built by men are often forgotten, he said.

> They should eternize, but the place
> Where shining souls have passed imbibes a grace
> Beyond mere earth; some sweetness of their fames
> Leaves in the soil its unextinguished trace,
> Pungent, pathetic, sad with nobler aims,
> That penetrates our lives and heightens them or shames.

"Beneath our consecrated elm," Lowell said, we see "bright clues of continuity." "The dumb earth hath memory . . . Past and Present commingle, fruit and bloom."

The Washington Elm was the center of the Revolution, the axis mundi. Washington drew his sword, and the American nation was born.

Washington was a deity. Washington was like Christ and Moses. His victories and retreats in battle were seen as having their corollary in Exodus. He delivered the citizens of New Canaan from bondage under King George. "Washington, in America, *is not a man but a God*," said Frenchman Gustav de Beaumont after a visit in the 1830s. An early American print, *The Apotheosis of Washington* (1800) shows him rising from Mount Vernon heavenward on clouds. Light shines down upon him as a cherub waits to bestow a laurel. In many biographies Washington is compared with Jesus, and referred to as "Him."

His mother is called "Mary, the Mother of Washington." In the Washington Memorial Chapel at Valley Forge, finished in 1917, there are two sets of thirty-six stained-glass windows. One set tells the story of Christ and the other of Washington. "Had he lived in the days of idolatry he had been worshipped as a god," said the *Pennsylvania Journal* in 1777.

In Lowell's ode, the general in his buff and blue uniform stands under the elm in golden light with a radiant halo.

> *The sun-flecks, shaken the stirred foliage through,*
> *Dapple with gold his sober buff and blue*
> *And weave prophetic aureoles round the head*

"Among the national sins of our country," said John Adams in 1812, is "the idolatrous worship paid to the name of George Washington by all classes and *nearly* all parties of our citizens, manifested in the impious applications of names and epithets to him which are ascribed in scripture only to God and to Jesus Christ. The following is a part of them: 'our Savior,' 'our Redeemer,' 'our cloud by day and our pillar of fire by night,' 'our star in the east,' 'to us a son is born,' and 'our guide on earth, our advocate in heaven.'"

Washington was the necessary hero. "Washington was more than a military leader: he was the eagle, the standard, the flag, the living symbol of the cause," said biographer James Flexner. He was the standard-bearer of virtue, said historian Garry Wills. Heroes were a part of the republican enterprise—they instruct, they hold society together. In a republic, a pantheon of heroes replaced the king.

"The eighteenth century aspired to make itself a hero factory; and in some measure it succeeded," said Wills in his Washington biography, *Cincinnatus*. Heroes, models of virtuous character, were needed if the republican experiment was to succeed, said James Madison. "Hero worship was not just an adjunct to this program," said Wills. "It was, for a while at least, at the center of the whole endeavor. If we cannot grasp that, we shall miss one large aspect of the revolutionary process."

"Washington was asked to be heroic, but heroically

restrained," said Wills. "Not only did he (and he alone) play a crucial role at *every* stage of the Revolution—in the war, the postwar period, the passage of the Constitution, and the establishment of a working government. He had to show a complete virtue, a complementarity of competing traits, that was asked of no other," said Wills. There may have been greater generals and "better philosophers of the republican ideal," but Washington steered a steady course, said Wills.

Parson Weems perfected hero worship in his early biography of Washington (ensuring that its many editions from 1800 to 1825 were best sellers). This is the book that gave us young George chopping down the cherry tree. ("I can't tell a lie, Pa; you know I can't tell a lie. I did cut it with my hatchet.") Washington's virtues, said Weems, were equal to a constellation of Greek, Roman, and Carthaginian generals, statesmen, and philosophers: "It is hardly an exaggeration to say that Washington was pious as Numa; just as Aristides; temperate as Epictetus; patriotic as Regulus; in giving public trusts, impartial as Severus; in victory, modest as Scipio; prudent as Fabius; rapid as Marcellus; undaunted as Hannibal; as Cincinnatus disinterested; to liberty firm as Cato; as respectful of the laws as Socrates." This pile of classical references is mostly lost on us today.

"More than most men, this man *was* what he meant to his contemporaries," said Wills. To us he is elusive. We can't reassemble Washington. We come up with the tight-lipped Gilbert Stuart portrait, with the cherry tree story, with Washington crossing the Delaware standing in a boatload of relics. "The man we can hardly find was the icon our ancestors turned to most easily and often," said Wills. To reassemble the Washington Elm we would need more than the old wood itself; we would need the young republic's belief in virtue and heroes.

We apprehend the new by comparing it with the old. Iron Horse. Horseless carriage. In a new nation, Washington was Moses, Jesus, and Socrates. The old, known stories were a way of facing the uncertainties of thirteen former colonies, which were deep in debt from the war, uniting under an elected president. Washington, the Bible, and antiquity furnished the bare room.

Washington was understood by some of the oldest stories. His story took the shape of the old religion, the worship in sacred groves of oaks that was common in Europe before Christianity. Oaks were powerful. The god of the "luminous sky," thunder and lightning, Zeus to the Greeks, Jupiter to the Romans, their highest god, sometimes spoke through a sacred oak. Under a sacred tree, Washington draws his sword and rides forth to glory.

Cambridge had its own sacred grove, a patriotic arboretum. One block northwest of the Washington Elm stood the Whitefield Elm. Under this elm in 1740, the Reverend George Whitefield, a Wesleyan evangelist, "moved a vast multitude by his eloquence." Across the common was the Election Oak, and in Harvard Yard there were the Class Tree and the Rebellion Tree, where students rallied to complain about their professors. On Mt. Auburn Street there were the Palisade Willows, celebrated in poetry by Lowell. And just around the corner from the common, on Brattle Street, was a blacksmith shop under a "spreading chestnut tree" immortalized by Longfellow, who walked by every day. Across the Charles River, Bostonians gathered under the Liberty Tree, which the British later cut down, and the Great Tree on the Boston Common. (When the British Army was encamped around this magnificent elm, General Gage forbid his men to cut it for firewood.)

"The college plain would be nothing without its elms," wrote Oliver Wendell Holmes Sr. "As the long hair of a woman is a glory to her, so are these green tresses that bank themselves against the sky in thick clustered masses the ornament and pride of the classic green."

Washington under his elm, Whitefield preaching nearby under his elm, and around the corner the village smithy working under the spreading chestnut tree. Nice neighborhood. A good place to raise a young country. I like these Cantabrigians with their groves of memory, their green monuments, their belief in marking time and the land with trees.

The Washington Elm spoke to people as did other named elms, oaks, chestnuts, willows, and landmark rocks. *What this tree has witnessed—if it could speak.* The Washington Elm did speak. It was a totem, a living symbol of belief. Totems carry the sacred life of a community. "The god of the clan [can] be nothing else than the clan itself, personified and represented to the imagination under the visible form of the animal or vegetable which serves as totem," said sociologist Emile Durkheim. But this definition is too limiting. It doesn't suggest the fluidity, the way in which the animate is everywhere, in the souls of animals, trees, and people.

The elm is Washington's representative. "Great events which mark epochs in history, bestow an imperishable dignity even upon the meanest objects with which they are associated," wrote L. L. Dame in 1884. "When Washington drew his sword beneath the branches, the great elm, thus distinguished above its fellows, passed at once into history."

The tree is ennobled by the general. It is a living monument. But the fascination with this tree says that it is more than that. It is a union, a mingling of man and tree, much the way people and animals traded places in the oldest stories. ("Sometimes they were people and sometimes animals and there was no difference," says one translation of an ancient Inuit song. "Nobody could explain this: That's the way it was.")

In a very satisfying way, the elm *is* Washington. It is Washington living in the landscape. His virtues are the elm's and the elm's virtues are his. No one would speak like this; they couch it in allegory. The elm represents Washington. We remember Washington by the elm. . . . But the poems, tributes, and the photos of the elm dressed up for the centennial tell us of a deeper identification. Washington is a tree. What could be nobler?

"I can't tell a lie."

Nearly two years shy of the 150th anniversary of Washington taking command, the Washington Elm fell over. Workmen from the parks department were cutting back two of the remaining limbs on October 26, 1923. "I removed one limb safely," reported the worker in charge, "and while removing the second . . . the whole tree toppled over onto the iron fence and cable of the Boston Elevated Railway, towards Mason Street, breaking one section of the fence and bringing the cable within fifteen feet of the ground." The sawed-off elm, looking like two arthritic fingers and a thumb, hung on the wire, caught in a death pose, the cruelty of the corpse, the whale washed ashore dead.

The police and the park workers held off a crowd of five hundred from seizing the fallen hero. ("Souvenir Hunters Battle with Police For Relics," said the front page headline in the *Boston Post*.) "One woman brought her own saw and threatened to use it on anyone who prevented her from sawing off a piece," said one report. One man approached the Superintendent of Parks and implored, "will you please save this tree. I am a representative of various historical societies and don't want another limb cut off that tree. I know an experienced tree surgeon who can save it by putting it back in the same position it formerly was in, placing a concrete wall around it and preserving it for future generations. I forbid you to put a saw on it."

He was too late; the Washington Elm had died that summer. When the limb was cut, the old tree had lost its balance, revealing that "the trunk was hopelessly rotted below the ground, a mere mass of punk." Not a single root held it in the ground. The elm had long been in decline, crowded by paving, sewers, and gas pipes, dropping big limbs in storms as elms will do. It had lost a large limb in 1872, and by the 1880s the pleasing fan of its crown could only be inferred from its lopsided shape. By the 1920s the senior citizen was shorn of many branches, with its "wounds smeared with tar, the hollows filled with cement, the remaining limbs braced with iron bands and rods, until it became a truly pitiable object," said one Cambridge resident. The Washington Elm was a worn rag doll of a tree, a favorite blanket or stuffed animal no one had the heart to toss out.

The Washington Elm had outlived almost all of the neighboring trees in Cambridge's "poetical arboretum." The White-field Elm had been cut down in 1871 to make way for traffic. "Earnest solicitation" had spared the tree for a few years. The "feeling of regret . . . at its final sacrifice was extensive." The "spreading chestnut tree" was felled in 1876, despite Long-fellow's protests, because "it imperilled drivers of heavy loads who passed under it." The children of Cambridge gave a chair made from the tree to Longfellow for his birthday.

The fallen elm was guarded through the night by police and park workers. The next day the park commissioners met and exonerated the workers (who had filed a typed report explaining how they had lost a national shrine on their watch). The elm was removed and "placed under lock and key" in a warehouse.

Experts counted the rings of the trunk. The elm had lived at least 210 years. Washington saw the tree when it was a vigorous sixty years old. As arborists had tried to explain over the years, this was not a survivor from the forest primeval. It had been planted some time after 1700 in a row of five other elms (including the Whitefield Elm) to provide shade for cows on the Cambridge Cow Common. The Washington Elm had stood on the common before the road was widened.

Cambridge sent "complimentary slabs" of the main trunk to the governor of each state and territory as "an object lesson in patriotism." Two gavels made from the smaller branches were also sent to each state's legislature. Some fraternal organizations also received a gavel. The cross-section that was used to date the tree was polished and sent to Mount Vernon. About 150 small blocks of wood, each identified with a metal plaque, were handed out over the counter, and a couple of hundred blocks were mailed all over the country. In total, Cambridge gave away about one thousand pieces. "There is no more of the tree available for distribution," said the park commissioners.

Two years later, almost to the day the Washington Elm had fallen, the secretary of the Cambridge Historical Society, Samuel F. Batchelder, read a paper, which he later reprinted as *The Washington Elm Tradition: "Under This Tree Washington First*

Took Command of the American Army." Is It True? The short answer was: no. The longer answer was: Are you kidding? It was a myth. The tree was real, but all the rest had been hung on it like the flags at the centennial.

Washington did not raise his sword under the "patriarch tree" as the crowd cheered. The grand ceremony on July 3 never happened. The troops never paraded for Washington. This was not an army for parades—four out of five officers didn't know the basic drills, and there was no official flag and few uniforms. Washington had to order his officers to wear ribbons so he could identify them. This was an army just two weeks after its defeat at Bunker Hill that was preparing for the next British attack. The troops had been ordered to stay at their posts. The day after Washington and General Charles Lee had arrived, they rode around Boston inspecting the troops and fortifications—miles from the elm.

The sword waving was another misconception, said Batchelder. A general doesn't take command by waving a sword like a magic wand. He takes command by exchanging official papers and studying the military situation. Besides, would a general reviewing troops hide under a tree from the hot sun "like a schoolgirl preserving her complexion?" asked Batchelder. "Would a commander on his first appearance before his men give such an example of trivial self-indulgence?"

The ceremony on the common was not mentioned in the official military and legislative records, the press, or in the numerous letters and diaries. The many camp journals kept by the soldiers record on July 3: "Nothing of importance this day." "Nothing remarkable." Washington's official report to the president of the Congress does not mention the "drumming and fifing, the parading and saluting that Cambridge loves to dwell upon," said Batchelder.

The event was testified to by old men and women breaking more than a half-century of silence with acute memories of that day. During the intervening years of anniversaries and July 4th orations, they had never thought to mention the festive review of the troops on the common. "We all know the story of the convivial octogenarian who before dinner could remember George Washington, and after dinner could remember Christopher Columbus," said Batchelder.

Many were assured of the story when "a venerable Mrs. Moore" pointed out the elm and described "the glories of the occasion, 75 years afterward," wrote L. L. Dame. "Fathers, who were eyewitnesses standing beneath this tree, have told the story to their sons, and those sons have not yet passed away. There is no possibility that we are paying our vows at a counterfeit shrine."

The first mention of Washington under the elm appeared in print more than sixty years after the general took command. In that account, Washington stands under the elm. In later accounts, he is on his horse, sword raised high. The story snowballed until Washington was up in the tree on a platform surveying the camps. Dorothy Dudley's diary describing the cinematic sweep of the "enthusiastic welcome" in 1775 was a forgery cooked up one hundred years later.

"Never was the advent or presence of mortal man a more complete and transcendent triumph," wrote Reverend Andrew P. Peabody in his introduction to the forgery. "Majestic grace and sweet benignity were blended in countenance and mien. He looked at once the hero, patriot, sage. With equal dignity and modesty he received the thunders of acclamation, in which every voice bore part."

The faked dairy inspired ever more inflated scenes of hero worship in school histories and magazines, which were often accompanied by "the most outrageous pictures," said Batchelder. "In these pictures the artists have allowed their 'historical imagination' to run amuck. Prancing steeds, dipping colors, dear little drummer boys, long rows of troops aligned to a hair's breadth, gorgeously uniformed, and presenting glittering arms with fixed bayonets, thrill every youthful heart, while smack in the middle of the front rank stands the Elm, with just room for Washington, flourishing his sword, to ride between it and his immaculate warriors." In one illustration Washington was "mounted apparently on a Shetland pony" while "enthusiastic ladies standing up in barouches . . . point out the hero to their children."

What had happened on that celebrated day when Washington rode into town? There was no "multitude thronging the plain around." Cambridge was nearly deserted. There were no "houses filled with interested spectators"—there was only one house nearby. It was raining so heavily that a small welcome had been canceled. At most General Artemas Ward and two or three aides may have ridden across the muddy common and sheltered under the large elm where the road met the common as they waited for the general. Washington arrived, tired and sick. A soaking wet, fatigued Washington meeting an ailing General Ward in a muddy road is not a scene for commemorative stamps, shoebuckles, rings, buttons, and memorial lockets.

People wanted to believe in the Washington Elm. Washington was a real man who had been changed into myth—the cherry-tree-chopping Cincinnatus-Socrates-Jesus—because nations begin in myths, not in facts. Rome, it was believed, was founded by Romulus and Remus, who were nursed by a wolf. For hundreds of years the Ruminalis Fig tree stood in the Forum, marking the site where the wolf had discovered the twin foundlings. A *ficus ruminalis* grows there today near a statue of the she-wolf suckling the twins.

Batchelder knew the power of the myth. "To discredit it would in manner impugn the faith of the city," he acknowledged. "To disbelieve it would somehow be not only unpatriotic but unfilial."

The story was a matter of faith, not facts. The believers were not swayed. "I think there is no doubt about it," said the historian general of the General Society of Mayflower Descendants. "I have never heard that there was any question," said the president of the Massachusetts Society of Colonial Dames of America. "I always believed it."

The Washington Elm was a seven-layer cake of myth and fraud, but those generations who believed in the tree were closer than us to Washington. When they gathered near the old elm to hear Lowell declaim the story of their new nation, they were standing in the right place, at the center of their belief in their hero and their faith in the future. They were standing at the axis mundi of a young republic.

The belief persists. A quick check of Web sites shows that homeschoolers are being told that it is a fact that the general took charge under the tree, while another site for homework has the "great elm" still standing "as a living monument." (This site relies on a 1904 textbook.) It is hard to part with the Washington Elm. In 1941 Massachusetts adopted the American Elm as its official state tree because of Washington. And for the national bicentennial, Cambridge used the elm as its symbol. (One visitor to a Boston bicentennial display was moved to say, "I have a piece of the tree where George Washington stood when he commanded the army! A piece of the tree, Jesus!")

The Cambridge Historical Commission gets calls all the time: We have a piece of the Washington Elm, is it worth anything? "We field more inquiries about the tree than about any other single Cambridge landmark, and each time we have to gently debunk the myth for another earnest history buff, often someone who owns a chunk of the tree," said Assistant Director Erika S. Bruner. (On the commission's Web site, this is one of their Frequently Asked Questions, even coming before: "Q: Do you have the original plans for my house? A: Probably not.")

After the elm fell, the "sacred spot" sprouted monuments, much the way a stump will send up shoots. An "authentic scion" of the elm was planted on the common in 1924, but died three years later. A second scion was planted in 1932 (the bicentennial of Washington's birth), this one taken from a tree at the University of Washington in Seattle. There was talk of putting up a statue of Washington on the site of the tree, or perhaps taking Boston's statue from the Public Garden. ("Not while I am mayor," answered Mayor James Michael Curley.) After World War II, the owner of a hotel near the Cambridge Common convinced the city to put up a new, larger marker, this one showing the troops parading past the general.

Today there are four memorials to the vanished elm. On the common there are the granite tablet (mistakenly credited to Longfellow), the grander post-World War II marker, and a modest-sized elm. Out in the middle of a busy intersection, looking like a manhole cover for a sewer, the tree's exact spot is marked. (You could be killed reading it.) This marker replaces an earlier one worn smooth by traffic.

The Cambridge Historical Commission marks the spot, not because Washington ever stood there, but because it's what people want to believe, said the director of the commission. This is a monument to a belief. It's a remnant of the totem.

When I saw the bronze manhole cover glinting in the morning light, I was reminded of the Navajo story of their origins. The Navajo know the exact spot where their people emerged from underground and began their journey here in the "Glittering World." The bronze marker looks like a navel, out of which Washington emerged and the nation was born.

The Bones
of the Earth

Pet Rocks

In New Hampshire, stone—granite—is what we have. We have lakes and mountains and five or six seasons of weather, but mostly what we have is granite. We live with granite, with large boulders shaped, we think, like elephants or monkeys or the Old Man of the Mountain. New Hampshire once fed itself with granite, quarrying the stone, or fed itself in spite of granite, moving miles of stone to farm. We have stones rising in our pastures and roads and cellars. Some of us wash and drink with water tainted with radon, a radioactive gas produced by uranium, which is sometimes found in dangerous levels in rocky places.

The Old Man of the Mountain was our pet rock, on road signs and souvenirs. It was a celebrated rock. Once everyone knew Nathaniel Hawthorne's story, or the dozens of other stories about the presiding spirit of New England, a certified wonder of the New World. People spoke of the "Great Stone Face" with that nineteenth-century mix of piety and boasting. The Old Man was a miracle and an advertisement. At the Philadelphia Centennial Exposition of 1876, New Hampshire's exhibit featured a large portrait of "the Profile" with the label: "Born—in the Creation. Resides—in Franconia." This rock, too, fed New Hampshire. The Old Man was a tourist destination. In the 1920s when Franconia Notch was threatened with clear-cut logging, there was a national outpouring of editorials, poems, and money. Children at an orphans' home sent in their pennies. Donations came from bankers and women's clubs, from Georgia, Illinois, and Texas. The Old Man was sacred; Franconia Notch was saved.

The Old Man was fussed over, his slipping forehead and scalp secured with large steel turnbuckles, cement, and epoxy—a 325-ton face-lift. He got the spa treatment annually; encroaching vegetation was cut back, and his epoxy waterseal was patched. But it was not enough. Some time late on May 2 or early on May 3, 2003, the rocks slid unseen off the mountain. It was international news. (I first heard about it on the BBC.) New Hampshire was shocked and disoriented. There was a flood of letters to the editor: That's my life that fell, people said. I saw him first when I was little, saw him every year. I said hello in summer and good-bye at summer's end. Put the Old Man back, many said. Lithic allegiances still live.

New Hampshire is, after all, the Granite State. (Our license plates should be flecked with greys, blacks, and bits of mica shine.) But we don't stand around talking about granite much. It would be like discussing the air. ("Sure is a lot of air out there today.") That's why I took note of a discussion of stone and art at the meat counter of the Hancock Cash Market.

An artist at the nearby MacDowell Colony had gilded one rock at the MacDowell Dam in 23-karat gold leaf. A gold-leafed rock seemed extravagant to the meat counter colloquium. Someone read aloud from the local newspaper: "This project is intended to enhance the appreciation of the MacDowell Dam," wrote Andrew Ginzel, the artist, in his proposal to the

Army Corps of Engineers. "It is meant to magnify the beauty of the innocuous, the ordinary materials from which the dam is built." This was greeted with laughter. It's been a long time since the "beauty of the innocuous" has come up in conversation at the meat counter. There was more. The gold rock was "meant to be there but not there, to have that quality of slightly otherworldliness," the artist said. The newspaper called the rock "an enigma in gold."

The language of proposals can be foolish, but that's not the artist's real work. If the Hancock Cash Market was funding "installation artists," I suspect that Andrew Ginzel would have pitched it differently. ("First, this gold rock isn't going to raise your taxes. Second, I won't be back here next year for more money.") I went to see the gold rock.

The gold rock is whimsical. It's a small object that you have to search for, and as you search you do study the piled rocks of the dam, not that they are worth your attention. I liked the gold rock. It had the intended effect. The shimmering rock is indeed "ethereal."

The gold rock can't compete with the Army Corps of Engineers' large installation art of the earthen dam. Dams are odd places, a landscape under arrest. The dam keepers at the MacDowell Dam work hard to make their dam educational and friendly to the public. They promote swimming and picnicking. They have renamed the reservoir the Edward MacDowell Lake. At the cul-de-sac turn around, the circle is marked as a sundial to follow a flag-pole's shadow. They do things like that, as if the dam keepers were some uncle who was a poor magician. (Pick a card, any card.) Why do the dam keepers try so hard? Is it that, outside of the big emergency, their job is boring? Dams are like army bases. They are erected for the fight you hope never comes. They are public hygiene, the dreary business of mass inoculations.

At the same time as the artist was gilding his rock, there was more talk of rocks in town. Howard Weston pointed out to

Jarvis Coffin, a Common Commissioner, that World War I is the last war commemorated on the common. One thrifty memorial listed the men who had served in the French and Indian Wars, the Revolution, the War of 1812, the Civil War, and "the World War." A new monument was needed to mark the sacrifices of veterans in World War II, Korea, and Vietnam.

The solution was straightforward. A committee of three decided that a granite boulder with a bronze plaque would be a fit monument. They drove around town and picked out the best looking rock. That's it. No call for architectural submissions, no obtuse guidelines and reviewing committees, no soldier statues, gunnery, arches, columns, walls, wreaths. . . . In a stroke they had disposed of the whole anguished business of creating a representational memorial. They had picked up a stone and planted it on the common, out-minimalizing the minimalists. Names, bronze, granite. The beauty of the innocuous.

The three men—Weston, Coffin, and Ray Pierce—began looking at rocks in the spring. By June, my neighbor Jarvis told me, "we started seeing rocks we have never seen before. Everywhere we went we envisioned potential candidates for 'the rock.' Try it sometime. New Hampshire, and particularly this area, has no shortage of candidates. Often when you have just found a beautiful rock, and you begin to look over the surface, unseen cracks and fissures appear. This went on for several months. There was a bit of debate over many rocks. Basically we'd see one and then another and another and continually ranked one over the other. We three closely examined perhaps thirty contenders, having driven by many more."

The winning rock, the one that was the right size and shape and color, had to be where a bucket loader could get at it. The first choice, weighing in at about seven tons, overwhelmed a huge bucket loader, pinning the bucket, and levering the rear wheels into the air. The prize was left where it sat right next to a rock that has the word FLAG STONES carved in it. (The name Henry James gave to Margaret Perry's farm. More lithic allegiances.) The bucket loader moved up King's Highway and plucked a five- to six-ton runner-up. The stone's broad, flatiron face has room for the bronze marker, and sadly, for wars to come.

The gold rock artist had the fancy talk, but he was not unlike our local installation artists on the common. Each singled out one rock for special attention with a valuable metal. In ancient belief, stones were the bones of the earth. Stones were animate. We are, at heart, ancients.

My neighbor's search had left him with an appreciation for the stonework of earlier generations. Looking at larger memorial stones in nearby towns, Jarvis wondered, "How the hell did they move those monsters in those days? Either they weren't in such a hurry, or they had many more people willing to help. Or that generation was so accustomed to moving rocks they didn't give it a thought."

Henry David Thoreau had asked a similar question. "We are never prepared to believe that our ancestors lifted large stones—or built thick walls . . . how can their works be so visible & permanent and themselves so transient!" Thoreau wrote in 1850. "When I see a stone which it must have taken many yoke of oxen to move lying in a bank wall which was built 200 years ago—I am curiously surprised, because it suggests an energy & force of which we have no memorials."

They moved a great deal of stone before the Petroleum Era. There are cellar holes with huge boulders snugly shouldered against each other, and handsome arch bridges built of stones set without mortar. There are about 240,000 miles of stone walls in New England, in one mining engineer's estimate. (By comparison there are about 70,000 miles of stone walls in Great Britain.) Built when the land was cleared, many of these walls are now concealed by the forest. New Hampshire's foresters have mapped every stone wall in the state south of the White Mountains. They were pursuing White Pine Blister Rust, which spread through currant and gooseberry bushes that grow along stone walls. The foresters produced stone maps. Shorn of the trees once more, New Hampshire looks like Ireland, thousands of small fields, a landscape ordered into rooms of three or four acres.

Brigham Nims moved some of that stone. Nims (1811-1893) was a Roxbury, New Hampshire, farmer, blacksmith, tailor, carpenter, and teacher. As his grandson said, "He could knit a mitten, make a shoe, or split stone in his granite quarry, aside from attending to his farm and civic duties." Brigham Nims kept a journal. Here's how the work went in the "stone lot":

October 1845:
14 Work for Caleb Goodnow splitting Stone on the Old Farm not very good success. . . .
15 Work for Caleb Goodnow splitting Stone. . . .
16 Work for Caleb Goodnow splitting Stone. . . .
17 Work for Caleb Goodnow splitting Stone. . . .

Sometimes Brigham notes how much stone he split:

24 Work in the stone lot split 34 f 12 in. . . .
25 Work in the stone lot split 50 f 18 in. . . .

Occasionally he allows himself a little more narrative:

30 Work in the stone lot with Stephen A.M. moveing stone and piling &c P.M. went to Keene by Mr. Batcheller's to see his stone ledge &c Stephen went with me saw the Irishmen work on the Railroad come through the Street saw the Dentist & c

And sometimes Brigham is paid for his hard work:

July 1847:
9 Went to Keene with 12 six in posts to Taft he paid me $3.60 and concluded that he would not have any more at present got the oxen shod on forefeet at Woods paid 50 cts

His brother Kendall Nims (1808-1876) was a farmer who tended an orchard, ran a sawmill, quarried his stone lot, organized singing schools, played violin, drew plans for the meeting-house, worked in his brother's store, and was active in the Whig Party. He also kept a journal, which he called "An Account of Labor:"

January 1840:

9   Went to Keene with Rufus & two loads of stone

10   Went to Keene with Rufus & two loads of stone

11   Went to Keene with Rufus & two loads of stone & loaded great stone

12   Sunday went to Meeting Mr. Rawson Preached evening singing

13   Went to Keene with Rufus & one load of stone the great one to Hammer evening a Meeting to Choose delegates to conventions

And so it goes for the next ten days: Four loads, two loads, four loads, two loads . . . with time out to cut wood, hear Mr. Rawson preach, fix the ox crib, and "break" a road (clear it of snow).

Stone, in these journals, is another crop. Splitting stone is like haying, or cutting wood. It's a heavy harvest. Days and days of moving stone by ox cartloads to Keene. Much of that granite rests in Keene in hearths, floors, sills, foundations, walls, and lintels. When you look upon the best stonework of those nineteenth-century workers, you realize they had a feeling for stone. They spoke its language. They fed themselves with granite.

Lithic Allegiance

"My uncle Derek says that he can hear stones speak, even call to him as he rummages through some old crumbled wall or farmer's stone dump on a search for special shapes," Kevin Gardner writes of his partner in stone wall building of the past thirty years. "His hearing is enhanced by humorous mysticism and the anthropomorphic respect most craftspeople develop for their materials, but it is also practical. For stones *do* speak with individual voices, from the tight ceramic clink of flat thin *dinner plates* to the compressive basso tap of two-hundred-pound granite *cannonballs. Sandstone* whispers and grinds, rotten *shale* knocks hollowly and falls apart, small mobs of field-picked pebbles rush from the breach in a pasture wall with a burst of energetic gossip.

"The stones in Derek's walls look comfortable. They appear to be laid in ways they might choose for themselves, if they had the choice. . . . Derek's walls are not spectacularly tight in the formal mason's way, but their fitting expresses a great and consistent sense of care, as though each stone had something to offer and none were unimportant. They have, if such a thing can be said about a stone wall, a kind of tenderness."

Gardner's family has an affection for stone. They move tons of stone by hand, carefully considering the place for each one. "Stone wall building has a kind of rhythm to it, a thoughtful, measured ritual of looking, moving, looking, stooping, lifting, moving; placing; and looking again." One short run of stone wall—one hundred feet long, two feet wide and three feet high—has fifty tons of stone. "It is not uncommon for New England wall builders to become nearly obsessed with shapes, able to recall for months or even years a particular favorite they once encountered, or one they needed but could not find. My aunt, Ruth Owen, once returned from a hiking trip laden with stones she had lugged down from the top of a mountain, just because their shapes appealed to her so irresistibly. Her only regret, she said, was that she had not been able to carry more," Gardner writes in his guide to building with stone, *The Granite Kiss*. The title is the family term for getting your fingers squeezed between two large stones. The family has its own stone language, describing stone shapes (cigars, baseballs, cantaloupes), stones that fit well (problemsolvers) and stones that disappoint (cheap seducers).

I enlist Kevin Gardner as my interpreter for a stone tour. I want to look at the stone arch bridges of Hillsborough, New Hampshire. In the nineteenth century, Hillsborough built bridges of stone. Almost everyone else was building wooden bridges, but the town had a selectman who believed in stone. The bridges were built without mortar, the stones raised in an arch as the Romans had done, built at first over a supporting wooden template. The stones in the arch are cut and carefully fitted, but on most of the bridges, the rest of the stone is piled as it would be on a stone wall. The bridges are one part ancient engineering, one part farmer's wall. They seem to be partially built, and partially found. Some of the bridges we examine are built right on the rock that sat there, an arch rising up from an irregularly shaped boulder. It's as if you were looking at the evolution of construction in one snapshot, from cave dwelling to engineering. All of this—the anonymous builders, the Roman arches supporting rough boulders—makes the bridges seem like survivors from antiquity, as if New Hampshire had been settled by Europeans in the Middle Ages.

We visit six bridges on a bitterly cold December afternoon. Our first stop is the Sawyer Bridge, a later bridge built from 1866 to 1867 by Reuben Loveren. The bridge is on the Hillsborough town seal and carried a heavy load of traffic until just a few years ago. Now bypassed, the double-arch bridge looks forlorn, set to one side like a junked car. The bridge connects a little-used parking lot of a tire warehouse store with nothing—it stops short of the other bank. The town plans a park here to correct this state-planned vandalism.

Gardner studies the bridge, examining the line of the arches and the way the stones have been laid above it. There are three kinds of construction: the rough cut blocks of the arch, the stonework above that is "just random fieldstone that was laid in more or less carefully—but not all that carefully," and a double row of rough blocks on top, which were added later. The granite in each layer of construction is from a different place. "This bridge surprises me," he says. "It's been played around with a lot." Over time, various maintenance crews lost faith in its mortarless construction, pointing some stones with cement. (We later learn that the northern arch had been jacked up fourteen inches in 1925 and reinforced with cement grout.) He shows me how the arch stones were improvised. Usually the construction of an arch was carefully planned, the arch stones selected in advance. "This one looks like they cut a whole bunch of stone that they knew they could use and then simply laid it in as it came to hand." There's one "troubling" spot, he says, where some stones have slipped on the inside edge of one arch on the upstream side. We speculate on 135 years of possible stresses from traffic, floods, and earthquakes. "Every once in a while enough of an earthquake comes along to toss the whole thing, so that for a split second the stones come apart on the way up, and then they just fall back together, but not exactly the way they were."

We drive to the next bridge, welcoming the warmth of the heated truck and discussing the construction. They would build a wooden arch and lay the stone over that. The side we see, the bottom, would be invisible during construction. The top of the stone is what matters: the stones must touch to lock in an arch. If you have seen drawings of how the Romans built arches, you have the construction manual. "There's no difference, except that the Romans cut their stone with some more care," Gardner says. "Some of that Roman stuff is breathtaking." In addition to his stonework and building his own post-and-beam house from scratch, Gardner is an equity actor, drama teacher, director, and theater festival judge. He has also published poems and songs, and he reports on the arts for public radio, sometimes reviewing plays. He judges each bridge we visit as a drama, appraising the builder's skill and delivering a verdict. His opinions and his diction, like his handshake, are forceful.

The second bridge on our tour is on the Second New Hampshire Turnpike in Hillsborough's Lower Village. The turnpike is a local dirt road for most of the way here. The bridge is disguised by new guardrails. You wouldn't know it's a double-arch stone bridge until you climb down the bank. This bridge's walls are a mix of rough cut stone and random boulders. Granite fence posts, which held the original guardrails, are an integral part of the construction.

"What I just love about this is the way the fence posts are built into the surface of the walls. That is stunning. It's just wonderful. And the keystone is a fence post—fabulous. That's the work of somebody who was thinking about how beautiful a thing can be and not just about making a bridge that would work." This bridge was built by James H. and Calvin A. Gould in 1864 for $100.

The river is so low that we can stand on the icy rocks underneath the arches. The southern arch has been messed with, showing patches of at least two kinds of cement. The arch had spread out and was dipping two feet. The state highway department carefully peeled the bridge back atop the southern arch and jacked it back up. The northern arch looks to be untouched, the stones separated by dark space where there would be mortar in other construction. "The stones appear to be floating in space. You think it's going to come right down on you. How can they stay there? This is just stunningly well done. This is just absolutely marvelous. When it's not pointed you can see the building that's in it," he says, his eyes fixed on the stonework.

Under the northern arch of the Second Turnpike bridge I see the majesty of these bridges, Hillsborough's lucky inheritance. Here a thousand or so tons of stone has a weightlessness like some shape-changing wall in an Escher drawing. It's like that moment when I have looked out at our pasture and seen my neighbor's horses racing each other for the joy of it. Their grace and fitness are near ideal. These stones have that kind of agility. "The line of the curve here is very assured. The regularity of the blocks that form the arch is just wonderfully done. This stone was all split with feathers and wedges. When you cut granite with feathers and wedges, it doesn't always do what you want. These stones are quite precisely shaped. Amazingly tight. I'll bet it was really thrilling to build one of these when you couldn't see the underside and then the taking away of the template must have been a big event."

"Is it going to stand?" I add. "You know it will—your craft and planning tell you that—but you don't know for sure."

"Right. It's almost like a magic act."

"Did the builders of this bridge love working in stone?" I ask.

"You have to think so. You can see it in their best work. There really is a kind of love in it. It's also speaking a language that was better understood by more people at the time that it was made. Because anybody driving along the Second New Hampshire Turnpike in 1875 who was a farmer, or anyone who was native to the countryside, would know good stonework from bad."

The next bridge we visit is primitive. On Gleason Falls Road we see a massive bridge that looks like a large stone dump. Where it crosses an island the walls swell out. The bridge has two arches of different sizes. One is quite small, more like a culvert. "If I was going to do an experiment and start trying to build arches, I'd start by building one like this because it has so much mass pressing down on that arch that it doesn't look risky. You're building less arch." The other arch is much larger and flattens out on top.

"That really is something because it's *so flat*. How much curve does a dry stone arch have to have to be okay?" he wonders.

"I don't know, but this arch makes you ask that question," I say. "You look at it and say, 'Wait a minute: Will that work?'"

The builders have further unsettled our notions of fitness by piling bigger stones on smaller stones in the arch. "I've never seen the stones get smaller as you got down from the top," Gardner says. "This one almost looks like it shouldn't be able to hold itself up."

"It doesn't win your confidence," I say, and we both laugh.

"Yet how long has it been here?" he asks.

This is the roughest bridge we have seen, built right on bedrock, and likely using the boulders from the small falls here. They cut as little stone as possible. Gardner thinks that this could have been one of the first stone bridges built in the early 1800s. He continues to judge it. "The sidewall building on this is almost disgraceful. It's a great big mess. They just loaded it up." Somewhere a Yankee is rolling in his grave, ashamed. His bad work has been found out, just as he feared on the evening he walked home from the job.

Our tour leads us to believe that there were two different classes of builders of these bridges, one which built with artistry as at the turnpike bridge, and another rougher group. One of these rough bridges, Gardner says, "looks like something thrown together by a gang of trolls." The rough stone bridges do have that feeling of belonging to a dark wood in a scary Brothers Grimm fairytale.

Gardner is puzzled by the crudeness of these bridges. The stone bridges were civic monuments, the work of many months' labor at a time when labor and capital were scarce. They were built when "the whole cult of improvement" took hold, expressing itself "in everything from the way fields are laid out to how the walls are by the house, so it's a little surprising to see that kind of randomness happen in a public structure of that era."

It may be that the arch itself was built by a separate team, an arch meister who supervised the cutting of the stones at the quarry, while the rest of the bridge was built with stone on the site. Or it may just be Yankee practicality—"We don't need to get beautiful here"—the same practicality that cast off the first bridge we saw, reducing it to a granite stump. "By the same token, if you're going to go to so much trouble to build the arch, why not make the kind of beautiful pattern in the face of the sidewall that we saw on the turnpike bridge? I mean, that's really nice. It doesn't take all that much more effort," Gardner says. It's the same question I have asked of the new thirty-three-million dollar five-mile-long bypass of Hillsborough. It's ugly, the earth mounded up as if the state's department of transportation were preparing to protect the road from a tank assault. Why not make it beautiful?—it wouldn't take much. The stone bridge builders may be more our contemporaries than we care to admit.

In late afternoon, with the sun diving toward the trees, we come to a diminutive bridge, as odd as that might sound as a description of thousands of tons of stone. It's a compact double-arch bridge, one lane wide. The bridge is easily seen at the intersection of two dirt roads. "This one's got whimsy. Look at the alleged fence posts. They're not even posts. They're leftover pieces that could just as well be in the side wall," Gardner says. The bridge is crowned with triangular pieces of stone, making it look like a child's drawing of the top of a castle wall. We refer to this one as the toy bridge. Actually this is called Carr Bridge for Jonathan Carr, a local counterfeiter who may have paid for the bridge with money he printed. The arches almost touch the road. "That helps give it a sort of lightness and a smallness."

"The arch stones are not as carefully cut as the Second

Turnpike bridge, but they're beautifully put together. Just wonderfully put together. The guy likes these toothy little triangles for his upper pieces. You can see that the one at the far end and the one in the middle almost look like they're two halves of the same stone." He's taking the bridge apart, weighing each stone and the builder's choices. (Earlier when I had asked him about how they would have moved a small stone weighing about 400 pounds, he said, "This is *not* a tough stone to move. This one you can drag or roll easily." I laughed. "You can—with bars. Roll this anywhere you want it to go.")

"If we built this bridge today by hand using similar methods, it would have a different feeling, wouldn't it?" I ask.

"Yes, I think it would have a different feeling at first. You'd probably have to build a few to get to do what this guy did. This is not the first bridge that this person built, you know," he says and laughs. "If you got a certain amount of practice at it and figured out the subtleties that don't show in the work, I'm sure you could get yourself to the point where you could produce this kind of work.

"But even if you built something that was *exactly* like this in its configuration . . . it would have no hope of looking precisely the same. You would then have to add the 175 years or so that this one has been standing there. The slight movements and alterations of the relationships among individual stones that occur to give it this intangible quality of permanence that it has now." We admire stonework because we believe in its permanence. He pauses, looking the bridge over: "It'd be fun to try, though."

Boneyards

Stone is of the earth, like us, but it is lasting. We want to marry our short days to stone. Seeking permanence, we mark our land, our graves with stone. Stone is "absolute reality, life and holiness," writes the historian of religion, Mircea Eliade. In the Bible, stone is a symbol of God or His presence. In the origin stories of many cultures, gods and people arise from stone—

the bones of the Earth Mother—and sacred stones bring fertility to sterile women. Stone is life and power concentrated, writes landscape historian J. B. Jackson. The cathedral builders chose stone for its "mysterious power" to link the heavens and the soul, our origins and destiny. "All that we ask of our landscape, [the Apostle] Thomas would have said, was a monument or two of stone, a series of landmarks to remind us of what we believe and of our origin and identity," writes Jackson.

But stone is a ticking clock. It is a slow clock, slow enough for us to believe in its constancy. Robert Thorson is a geologist who loves old stone walls. He's put his ear to stone walls and heard them running back to the sea. ("The crackling of an ice cube" followed by a "tiny snap" and "a tiny sprinkling noise . . . a single grain detaching and falling somewhere within the wall.") He's put his hand on old stone walls and felt the earth moving.

"One night last spring I placed the palm of my hand on a lumpy granite boulder on the derelict wall surrounding my property. It was still warm . . . I felt a tiny seismic impulse followed quickly by a faint, almost metallic clunk in the distance. Puzzled at first, I suddenly realized what had happened. A stone in the wall had shifted its position, falling down slightly to the underlying stone. Perhaps a tree root had finally thrown the wall out of balance, or a mineral grain between two stones had given way to a century's worth of pressure, or the soil was shrinking back from the heaving of winter.

"Over the centuries, stone walls have come apart grain by grain . . . The fate of nearly every mineral crystal on earth is to dissolve, to be washed to the sea, and to be recycled back into rock or some other organic form." Thorson calls it "organic redemption." We drink stone walls. Stones build bones.

"We need physical contact with the earth's crust," says Thorson. "We must be able to *feel* our way through time." The landscape ticks, stone walls shift, arches of granite leap up in an earthquake and fall back to resume their labors. The memorial stone my neighbors have set out on the common is a clock.

The Grief
Police

The Beaulieus stand behind the grave of seventeen-year-old Jenifer. They face the camera united: father in the back, his wife alongside their surviving daughter, and in front, a five-year-old nephew. A two-year-old niece sits to one side of the polished black granite memorial: "BELOVED DAUGHTER, JENIFER L. BEAULIEU, DEC. 13 1978-JULY 9, 1996." Above the inscription three images are carved in the stone: a dancer with the words "Sweet & Sassy," an angel blowing a horn, and a portrait of their smiling daughter.

They have decorated the grave with two colorful banners, one on each side, a butterfly on one and sunflowers on another. Next to the flags, just above the headstone, they have hung four wind chimes. Close by the headstone are two large red-glass vigil lights, and on a shelf just below the inscription they have lined up more than a dozen small objects, including a teddy bear and a yellow smiley-face candle. On the ground are two wooden planters with flowers, a ceramic rabbit, a small cross, and two large plastic flowers with petals that spin with the wind. This display has brought the family to the front page of the local daily newspaper. "An emotional issue," it says over this portrait of mourning.

Some people were offended by the Beaulieu's memorial. "Good Lord, what's that mess?" they said. "It looks like a circus." At first people kept their comments to themselves and let it be. Marlborough, New Hampshire, is a small town, and in small towns, words easily wound. But by the first Memorial Day after the Beaulieus had lost Jenifer, a visitor from Connecticut had complained. After that, the cemetery trustees faced a "chain reaction" of public hearings, headlines, and sharp words.

Volunteering to serve as a cemetery trustee is usually a no-profile job, one of the many ways in which small towns are quietly, almost invisibly, tended. Before the Beaulieus had raised their banners and wind chimes, the three trustees' biggest problem was foxes. Foxes steal the small American flags set out for veterans' graves. They run all over with the flags, or play tug of war. Foxes also have an eye for plastic flowers. People call the trustees to report that someone has stolen their flag or flowers, and they have to tell them about the foxes.

The Beaulieus had not violated cemetery regulations. No rules prohibited their display. No rules were needed; everyone had once honored the dead in a similiar fashion. To some, the Beaulieus had breached what was unspoken and understood.

"People used to respect a cemetery," said Alphonse Depres, a cemetery trustee. "You didn't go in for a lot of ballyhoo or fancy decorations. Twenty-five, thirty years ago, I don't think anybody would have thought of putting up all these flags and whirligigs. I think they felt a deeper respect."

But the Beaulieus were showing their respect. "We're up there every day, trudging through snow in the winter just to visit and make sure her grave looks perfect," said Jenifer's mother, Cynthia. "For someone who only goes up on Memorial Day, to tell us what to put on our grave just isn't fair."

"This is the only way we have left to show our love for Jenifer," Cynthia said. "She loved bright colors and music, so we keep the grave bright and alive."

The cemetery trustees held a public hearing to write new rules, and met, head-on, love and death. The family's friends packed the room. The Beaulieus have lost their daughter and this is how they are treated? they said. This is how they show their love. Anyone who disagreed, who thought it was inappropriate, didn't dare speak, said Depres. "They would have been crazy. It's rather intimidating." Depres had seen conflict serving on the school board, but nothing like this. "I took a lot of heat," he says. The meeting was halted after an hour.

The other two cemetery trustees quit shortly after the meeting. Other towns took the confrontation in Marlborough as a "wake-up call" and rewrote their cemetery rules. (Marlborough approved new rules, but the Beaulieus were allowed their memorial.) The story kept spreading. It went out on a wire service, and Depres got a call from a reporter in California: "What kind of ogre was I to be banning decorations?"

This small-town upset had struck a nerve. In one evening, in a small room packed with emotion, the Beaulieus and the cemetery trustees were confronting the American way of death. The Beaulieus, on the front page of the newspaper, standing behind the decorated grave, were facing down not only grief but history.

Grief is a tightly regulated emotion. Throughout history Americans have dictated the rituals of mourning. We have had more to say about the funeral and the graveyard than the town common, the highway, or the front lawn. Public spaces have often been a private matter, but the grave, your last bit of real estate, is subject to detailed community review. In death we all get into line, or at least we used to.

The troubles in Marlborough's cemetery are representative. The episodes repeat in a set form across the country, and several instances can stand for many. A few examples:

In Columbus, Ohio, cemetery trustees have asked the family

of a sixteen-year-old killed in a car accident to remove the decorations surrounding his tear-shaped headstone, including five pinwheels, a can of Mountain Dew, toy soldiers, artificial flowers, stuffed animals and dolls, money, candles, necklaces with angel pendants, two hanging plants on six-foot-tall hangers, and an American flag on an eight-foot pole. Special decorations have been added for holidays: a six-foot-tall plastic Easter bunny in a lawn chair, a motion-activated noisemaker for Halloween, and a miniature Christmas tree. The teenager's friends hung a birthday greeting on a nearby fence in three-foot-high letters made of plastic cups.

As in Marlborough, the family has posed behind the decorated grave in a local newspaper, and once more the trustees are in the awkward role of defending "good taste." The trustees have only removed the birthday greeting, while asking the family to consider the sensibilities of other mourners. "Our hearts go out to the family, but there has to be a point where you say, 'This is not reasonable,'" said one trustee. "This has to remain a place of dignity."

In New York, the Catholic church put an end to these displays. The Cemetery of the Holy Rood had let toys, teddy bears, and pinwheels accumulate in the children's section, even though it was against the rules. "How come this section looks so bad?" some visitors asked. A cemetery director found one grave decorated for Halloween with fake spider webs, vials of fake blood, and a pumpkin with a knife sticking in it. The Diocese of Rockville Centre sent out six hundred letters announcing that the rules would be enforced. Parents were given a deadline to retrieve the objects. Some parents had chosen Holy Rood because the decorations made the cemetery seem less forbidding. "It's a shock enough that you have to bury a baby," said one mother, who like others brought Christmas, Easter, and birthday presents to her infant son's grave. "At least you should have a nice place to visit, a place for family that doesn't look so cold."

After the church had banished toys, it revised its rules and regulations. Holy Rood's rules are typical. The rules begin: "A strict observance of proper decorum in dress and action which should characterize such a sacred place is asked of all visitors."

The planting and decoration regulations are extensive: "Single and Double Graves: Only annual flowers may be planted within a semi-circle of 18" in front of the monument. . . . No shrubs or bushes, vines, perennials, climbers, hedging or growing boundaries are permitted. Any such planting will be removed. For flush marker graves, no permanent plantings are permitted. . . .

"Three Grave Plots and Larger: Shrubs and bushes are permitted. . . . Before planting any such shrubs, the Cemetery office should be consulted in order to be sure that your planting will conform to the type of shrub permitted and to its maximum size. . . .

"In order to protect the safety of field employees, wooden crosses, pinwheels, glass jars, statues, shells, vigil lights, balloons, marble chips, planters, edging and bric-a-brac of any description are not permitted. . . . Please note that Mylar balloons will stain the monument. Any article of this nature placed on plots will be removed without notice.

"Artificial flowers will be permitted *only during the winter months. . . .*" And so on.

Children's graves are the front line, the bell ringer in the newsroom, but they are not the only contested space in cemeteries. For more than a decade, families at the Boca Raton Municipal Cemetery have been setting up crosses, statues of Jesus and the Virgin Mary, and the Star of David. They have also planted ground coverings and borders. The city reversed course, directing the families to remove the monuments and plants or they would be destroyed in a few months. The cemetery regulations only permitted markers flush to the ground. Vertical religious symbols violated the rules and were a hazard to the workers, said the cemetery. Some 400 families, backed by the American Civil Liberties Union, sued the City of Boca Raton.

The International Cemetery and Funeral Association filed a friend of the court brief contending that the families knew that Boca Raton is a "memorial park," a cemetery restricted to flush markers. This creates an open, lawn-like park. A "vertical marker" is as out of place in a memorial park as a horse and buggy on a freeway. "Integrity of design drives the memorial park concept," said the association. "If individual lot owners become entitled to ignore cemetery regulations to do whatever they wish in the name of religious beliefs, they would effectively disenfranchise the rights of all the other lot owners and undercut the cemetery's ability to properly manage its grounds, resulting in a chaotic cemetery environment."

The families lost the first round. The judge upheld Boca Raton's rules, noting that the families don't own the cemetery plot, just a "right to burial" (or legally speaking, an "easement").

In Massachusetts, there is a battle that presents a collision of loyalties. The Westfield Veterans Council has sued the Diocese of Springfield. For fifty-seven years the veterans have set out American flags from Memorial Day to Veterans Day in St. Mary's Cemetery. When the Diocese of Springfield took over the cemetery from the parish, they were determined to remove 1,600 flags. Under the new rules, flags are only allowed for a week before and after Memorial Day and Veterans Day. The church and the veterans went to court. "It's something that we just have to fight for," said Richard Trusty, a seventy-four-year-old World War II Navy veteran. He has family and friends buried there who have served their country. The best man from his wedding is buried in St. Mary's. "He's a veteran, and the smallest thing they've given him is this little flag. I know the flag is only a symbol, but it means something to me. They can't just pull it up."

I know it's only a symbol, each mourner says, but it's all I can offer. Why do you refuse me in my hour of grief?

The modern cemetery is a triumph of decorum. If there is one constant in the three-hundred-year-long evolution of the American way of death, it is that too much grief is in bad taste. "Gaudiness is often mistaken for splendor, and capricious strangeness for improvement," said Adolph Strauch in 1869.

Strauch is considered the founder of the modern cemetery. He had tamed the lavish mausoleums and monuments of the Victorians, but he could be talking about pinwheels and balloons.

Mourners have been chastised for showy funerals and monuments in the long campaign to police grief. As funerals became more elaborate in the eighteenth century, the Massachusetts State Legislature in 1753 restricted funeral spending. Some families in New York dissipated "at least a fourth part of their whole fortune" on a "pompous interment." Young men of wealth saved money for their final show. "There is, perhaps, no article in which we carry our prodigality to higher excess than that of our funerals," said one critic. In the nineteenth century, cemetery rules became more specific. The first rules were tentative. Laurel Hill in Philadelphia published a "leave to suggest to lot-holders" in 1836 asking that graves be marked with only a low headstone but no footstones or mounds. However, they had "no wish to interfere with individual taste."

A few years later in 1839, Brooklyn's famous Green-Wood Cemetery published a more demanding "Rules and Regulations." On flowers Green-Wood had much to say: "Nothing coarse and incongruous with the object and the place should be chosen. Those which are delicate in size, form and color should be preferred. Such as are simple and unobtrusive, and particularly those which are symbolical of friendship, affection, and remembrance, seem most fitting to beautify the Place of Graves."

"Good judgment and taste should prevail," said Green-Wood's rules. The nineteenth century can seem like one long harangue about good taste and proper behavior in housekeeping and hygiene, in speech public and private, at the theater and at the grave. In 1846 the landscape gardener Andrew Jackson Downing criticized excessive plantings, monuments, and "vulgar iron railings, posts, chains, balustrades, etc . . . for the most part barbarous and cockneyish in their forms." In 1861 Frederick Law Olmsted despaired of "the grossest ostentation" of many cemetery visitors. And in the twentieth century,

Park and Cemetery magazine complained that the newest Americans had not signed on with the program. Immigrants had to be educated to properly bury their dead. "Some of the people bring their own customs and prejudices from their native country and it seems morally impossible to get them to conform to improved American ideas of cemetery management," the trade journal said in 1912.

"The weird taste of the foreign element for freakish monuments" would not be allowed, said one cemetery superintendent. "The improvement in cemeteries must be conducted under one general plan *dictated* by *educated taste,*" said another superintendent. Who would tell the mourners? "How am I going to convince an illiterate foreigner, full of sentiment and emotion, that a 'thoroughly studied composition in the tablet type with the decor in the current modern influence' is better for the grave of the child than the carved lamb for which the soul of him yearns?" asked a monument dealer. "Am I supposed to tell him that he is a darn fool and ignorant for being so sentimental? Am I supposed to give him a high school education and intensive course in the appreciation of beauty while my competitor sells him the lamb?"

The anguished public meetings about excessive decorations, the lawsuits about flags and crosses, are an American tradition. Early American funerals reflected "the tension between the private nature of death and the public display of grief, which would manifest itself throughout American history," says historian David Charles Sloane. Too much grief was "mere selfishness," said the funeral industry. "The deepest grief is the quiet kind."

In the pursuit of decorum, the family lost control of the funeral. The dead were removed from the living. Distance is the essential indicator in the history of mourning. At different times in history, the dead have been banished, or they have been present daily, arm in arm with the living.

The ancient Romans buried the dead outside the city in crypts they would visit. By the Middle Ages in Europe, the dead were buried under cathedrals and churches. The richest patrons bought a spot near a martyr or a saint. Strivers had to settle for the northern wall (bad things, like the Vikings, came from the north), or a spot in the churchyard. Paupers were buried in unmarked graves. The dead were present at the center of a community's life.

This is how we began to bury our dead in America. Church graveyards were crowded and graves were reused. By 1800 Trinity Church in lower Manhattan had buried almost one hundred thousand people on less than five acres, the ground level rising several yards above the street. Churchyards were rough places with tightly packed, wavering lines of graves. "The confused medley of graves seems like the wild arrangement of some awful convulsion of the earth," said one observer in 1805. Graveyards were used for markets, fairs, and to graze animals.

After the American Revolution, reformers began to call for the dead to be buried outside the city. Graveyards were unhealthy and ugly, they said. "In the common imagination, graveyards were one step removed from Heaven, and a half step from Hell," writes historian John R. Stilgoe. Burials were banned in lower Manhattan in 1823.

The new graveyards outside the city were called cemeteries, from the Greek for sleeping chamber, a temporary resting place to await Judgment Day. The dead were a carriage ride or a railroad trip away. Families still buried their dead, preparing the body and holding the wake at home. But with the cemetery further away and more people living in apartments, undertakers (who built coffins) expanded their services. The first funeral homes opened in the 1880s, and in time undertakers became funeral directors, the coffin became a "casket," and funerals became more formal.

The next reform came from a French import. The opening in 1804 of Père-Lachaise in Paris broke with one thousand years of Western history. Père-Lachaise was the first burial ground designed as a landscaped garden. It became a tourist attraction. One American visitor reported "feeling a solemn yet sweet and soothing emotion steal over the senses."

Père-Lachaise was also the first cemetery to lease perpetual burial rights. Before Père-Lachaise only the bones of royalty could rest undisturbed. Commoners had rented shallow graves for six to twenty years.

Mt. Auburn in Cambridge, Massachusetts, was the first American cemetery to imitate Père-Lachaise and it set the fashion for rural, or garden cemeteries as they were called. Mt. Auburn was "a village of the quick and the silent, where Nature throws an air of cheerfulness over the labors of Death," said an editorial at its opening in 1831. In rural cemeteries the "gloom of death cannot sadden the hearts of the living," said one of the thousands of visitors. "A glance at this beautiful Cemetery almost excites a wish to die," said a Swedish visitor to Mt. Auburn. By 1860, 140,000 annually visited Laurel Hill, and nearly a half million visited Green-Wood. The cemeteries sold guides suggesting tours. The rural cemeteries are the ancestors of Central Park and other urban parks.

The rows of headstones were replaced with obelisks, columns, urns, statues, crypts and mausoleums, in the Classical, Gothic, and Egyptian styles—Parthenons, medieval churches, and pyramids—set on winding drives under trees and sometimes by small ponds. Mt. Auburn was also an arboretum. The family monument commanded the cemetery, each one proclaiming wealth in the kingdom now, and to come in the life hereafter. The symbolism was elaborate: an anchor signified hope, ivy for memory, poppy for sleep, oak for immortality, acorn for life. One guidebook listed twenty-six different symbols, an alphabet of death and resurrection. "Death, so full in itself of dreariness and terror" had been "softened down into the grateful and peaceful idea of sleep," said one writer in a Christian magazine.

Harriet Martineau, an English Unitarian touring America in the 1830s, encountered this theology of sleep and rebirth on her visit to Mt. Auburn: "A visitor from a strange planet ignorant of mortality, would take this place to be the sanctum of creation. Every step teems with the promise of life. Beauty is about to 'spring up out of ashes, and life out of the dust': and

Humanity seems to be waiting, with acclamations ready on its lips, for the new birth."

The rural cemetery was a show. Adolph Strauch thought it had gotten out of hand. There were too many monuments, trees, and twisting picturesque roads. The father of the modern cemetery disciplined grief. In 1855 Strauch became the Superintendent of Spring Grove Cemetery in Cincinnati. He restricted monuments, removed trees to open views, and took down the fences around family plots, creating the "landscape-lawn" cemetery. Strauch favored symmetry. He organized the cemetery "on a scientific plan." Individual headstones were limited to six inches in height. Family monuments had to meet cemetery guidelines and review. Lot holders could no longer choose plantings. Strauch ousted their private gardeners and the cemetery took over landscaping. Strauch, a Prussian gardener, enforced "correct taste." He was vilified by some lot holders and the Cincinnati newspapers as an anti-American heathen. His life was threatened. In time Spring Grove came to be internationally admired. A French commission touring the world's cemeteries and parks called it the "most beautiful of all cemeteries."

In California, the cemetery—a French fashion reformed by a Prussian gardener—received its next makeover. In 1913 Hubert Eaton took over Forest Lawn Memorial Park in Los Angeles. At Forest Lawn the headstone was eliminated. Only bronze tablets flush with the ground are allowed. (They must be purchased from the cemetery.) There are no family monuments.

Eaton made Forest Lawn a consumer service, modeled on real estate and insurance. Forest Lawn advertised and sold "pre-need" funerals and grave sites. But they did not just sell a grave or a coffin, they sold "advice." They were death planners. It was a package deal. The cemetery had been rationalized; it was like a suburban subdivision with a limited range of options.

At Forest Lawn each section is a garden themed to a sculpture: Loving Kindness, Celestial Love, Murmuring Trees, Vale of Hope, Enduring Faith, Court of Freedom (for veterans). The price for a plot increases near the garden feature. (In real estate you create "frontage": land on a lake, park, or with a view.)

Forest Lawn is the most visited private cemetery in America. Since the 1920s most new cemeteries have been memorial parks. At Forest Lawn visitors can take a two-hour tour to see the copies of the Michelangelos: Pieta, Last Supper in stained glass, and David. (David's figleaf was removed in the 1970s.) The cemetery is a popular place for weddings. Eaton wanted Forest Lawn to be a happy land. "Today religion is gladsome, radiant, it speaks in terms of the Beatitudes, of joyousness, and the smiling Jesus," said Eaton. "I therefore know the cemeteries of today are wrong because they depict an end, not a beginning. They have consequently become unsightly stoneyards, full of inartistic symbols and depressing customs. . . . I shall try to build at Forest Lawn a great park, devoid of misshapen monuments and other customary signs of earthly Death, but filled with towering trees, sweeping lawns, splashing fountains, singing birds, beautiful statuary, cheerful flowers. . . . Forest Lawn shall become a place where lovers new and old shall stroll and watch the sunset's glow . . . where school teachers bring happy school children . . . a place where the sorrowing will be soothed and strengthened because it will be God's garden." Eaton searched for a smiling Jesus statue, but never found one that pleased him.

The American cemetery had evolved from the terror of death to sleep, from gloom to "gladsome" joy in Pacific sunshine. In the memorial park, said one park promoter, "there is no note of sadness. The flowers fling their fragrance far and wide, the fountains tinkle merrily and it is a beautiful park and the onlooker enjoys it." Eaton instructed mausoleum architects that "insofar as possible all evidences of death should be eliminated and that this building should be a creation of art." Memorial parks developed new techniques to hide the dirt of fresh graves and avoid the mounding and sinking of graves, which marred the old burial grounds. At a memorial park, the lawn is a level putting green. (Even caskets were redesigned so that the dirt falling on the lid did not make a "doleful sound.")

"We are very far here from the traditional conception of an adult soul naked at the judgement seat and a body turning to corruption," Evelyn Waugh wrote in *Life* magazine in 1947. (Waugh would satirize Forest Lawn in his novel, *The Loved One*.) At Forest Lawn "the body does not decay; it lives on, more chic in death than ever before, in its indestructible Class A steel-and-concrete shelf; the soul goes straight from the Slumber Room to Paradise, where it enjoys an endless infancy."

There are no epitaphs at cheerful Forest Lawn. You will not find a headstone, as you would in a New England graveyard, with a skull and cross bones and the scolding epitaph: "Death is a debt to nature due, which I have paid, and so must you." You will not see a monument depicting the body eaten by worms, and the soul risen to paradise, as in medieval Notre Dame. Nor will your visit be troubled by piles of bones and skulls as in an eighteenth-century Roman chapel. Forest Lawn does not welcome visitors with an alabaster statue of a desiccated corpse at the entrance as the largest ancient European cemetery, the Cemetery of Holy Innocents in Paris, did in the sixteenth century.

"The memorial park," said one park owner, "breaks down the strangeness of the cemetery." The old funereal monuments are embarrassing to the cemetery professional. One cemetery administrator was asked about the statue of the Grim Reaper in Chicago's Bohemian National Cemetery. "I think it is kind of atrocious," he said. "A lot of people call it the statue of death. Of course, we all know we are going to die. I don't know why you want to have that."

In the twentieth century, cemetery design had one goal: "the interdiction of death in order to preserve happiness," says the French historian Philippe Aries.

Today's cemetery is a corporate landscape, closer to the gated-private enclave than to the churchyards and town cemeteries that preceded it. "We are manufacturers," one "cemeterian" reminded his colleagues in 1944. "Instead of coke, slag, pig-iron, etc., we take ground, fertilizer, seed, shrubs, trees, flowers, water, stones, top dressing, etc. and with equipment and men we manufacture a 'product' known as a cemetery. Then we divide this product into individual lots—'packages'—and there you have it."

And there, more and more Americans say, you can leave it. "Americans have become increasingly indifferent to the cemetery as a sacred space or as a community and cultural institution," writes David Charles Sloane. "The cemetery's role as a repository of the history and memories of the local community is fading."

The graveyard has been tamed into a memorial park and banished to the farthest possible precincts. Some cemeteries are in financial trouble, others are neglected or abandoned. Developers and city planners covet the valuable real estate used by cemeteries, such as Seattle's Lake View Cemetery overlooking Puget Sound. A report for the Department of Housing and Urban Development in 1970 suggested that new cemeteries be placed under highways, near airports, and on reclaimed landfill.

After a motorcycle accident killed a young man on a nearby state highway, his friends erected a small cross wreathed with flowers. I would see his friends there by candlelight in the evening, with their heads bowed. They seemed so exposed, as if the walls of their house had fallen. I have seen these roadside shrines in many parts of the country. They are a cousin of the banners in the cemetery, and less visibly, the homemade ceremonies for spreading ashes in a beloved place.

If cemeteries won't give people permission to grieve, that sorrow will find expression in another place on the landscape. At a roadside shrine no one is going to tell you not to leave plastic flowers or a bottle of your buddy's favorite beer. And what's more, you can see him every day as you go by. He is not off in section 8, row 14, in the Garden of Happy Death. You have kept the dead nearby, just as we used to, and as some cultures still do.

The roadside shrine upends three centuries of evolution in the graveyard. It puts the dead in our path. These homemade shrines are anguished cries: This is the last place that this person who I loved was on earth. They are not mediated by the clergy and the "death care industry." This is grief that has leapt the fences beyond the little pallid memorial service and the factory-standard marker.

Outside Atlanta along a busy highway, a white cross, nearly seven feet tall, made of two-by-fours marks where twenty-three-year-old Nancy Benedit was crushed when a tractor-trailer ran head-on into her car. "She was our only daughter, a great kid and always happy," says her father, Robert. "She was the type of person you want to have around when you're having a bad day. Because she could surely turn it around for you." Her parents and grandparents tend the shrine, bringing new stuffed animals and balloons, replacing the artificial flowers, and giving the cross a new coat of paint. "This is where she had her last minute of life," says her mother, Virginia. "This was her last home."

"Like so many things, our idea of death and burial changed during the sixties," says Gary Laderman, a professor of religion at Emory University. "The simple funeral-home burial had once been universal across all classes, races, and religions. But suddenly one could experiment. There was a real surge in alternative rituals—cremations, burial societies, roadside shrines, political movements like Mothers Against Drunk Driving. You get a series of improvisations, trying to perpetuate the presence of death."

The cemetery decorations and roadside shrines are rebellions, a protest against mourning without representation. For several generations death has been overseen by strangers. The mourners are handed a list of rules, told not to interfere, and reminded that they do not own their family burial plot. Feeling the chill, some families have hung out the banners. Parents, in particular, feel as if they are abandoning their children to something regimented and corporate. The pinwheels and flags are a new symbolism returning to a cemetery that has been shorn of its angels, lambs, grieving women carrying urns, broken columns, extinguished torches, and epitaphs.

The families at the graves with the flags and teddy bears are asking us to reconsider, to call off the grief police. Our cemeteries could be otherwise: we could have mandated pinwheels and flags, or the cooking of meals for the dead on one day each year. It looks messy, people complained at the Cemetery of the Holy Rood. Unfortunately no one answered: Yeah, well, grief is messy.

Cemeteries are for the living. The dead, the deceased, the departed, the loved ones, they are gone. We mark the graves, mow the grass, leave flowers and stones, or flags and candles, for we the living.

The Mont Vernon, New Hampshire, cemetery is in the center of town. The tall headstones of the earliest burials up front along Main Street are shaded by magnificent old maples. The maples are planted close on a narrow lane, giving a casual walk the dignity of a procession. The maple shaded lane leads to the newest part of the cemetery, recent burials on a treeless plain in the model of the landscape lawn cemetery. The Wilson grave stands out. The deaths of two teenage girls, five weeks apart, has been memorialized in a small area behind their headstone where a bench faces two little angels watching over the girls' names in granite, Angel and Cassie. A basket with cloth flowers hangs above the angels. In front of the headstone are well-tended flowers.

I have come to Mont Vernon, a small town of 2,200, to meet Al Ryder, a cemetery trustee and a retired computer science engineer. He points out two other graves, one for an infant, and one for an eighteen-year-old killed in a "car accident not of his own making."

When someone my age dies it is to be expected, Ryder says. "None of us has a permanent ticket here. Between the age of sixty and the age of 110 we're sooner or later going to come here. When a child dies it does hit me. It hit me when this one died three years ago," he says, referring to the teenager killed in the accident. "Just before I first came aboard, we had the death of an infant, and about that time we had the death of two teenage girls. The owners of that plot have violated every rule in our book. And that is something that cemetery trustees always face. By and large, unlike some branches of the government, we tend to be patient. On all of the graves we will pretty much allow immediate decorations that just are completely unreasonable in terms of long term maintenance. But with time things can be improved.

"The infant's grave: that once had whirligigs and balloons on sticks and things of that sort above it. They're not there now. We never told them to take them away. They're just not there.

"On the other hand, the grave of the two teenagers: They put in things that were even more difficult in terms of mowing and maintenance. And ordinarily it would be about time, after this many years [eight], to call the owner and talk about making a few changes. But about a month ago I was here on some other work, and while I was here, a woman drove in, walked over to that site, sat there in meditation for awhile, and then began to take care of the flowers.

"There's no way that I'm going to walk over to her and say, 'Hey—get that stuff out of here.' You're not about to walk over to someone in grief and start talking about rules and regulations.

"The conflict that arises is that you publish the rules, and if you don't enforce them, the next person comes along and says, well, so-and-so did it. I'll do it. And you don't have a good argument against that."

Ignoring the rules irritates the professionals. Jeff Snow is the superintendent of Edgewood Cemetery in Nashua, New Hampshire. As the secretary and treasurer of the New Hampshire Cemetery Association, he has sought to impress the membership that if there's a rule, it needs to be consistently enforced. When you suddenly apply the brakes and announce that the rules will be enforced, people will be upset. This is the basic scenario that, in different cemeteries, has set parents and veterans against the Catholic Church. Snow has organized a panel discussion for the association's annual meeting: "Why Rules?" A few years ago on a similar panel, Snow and Ryder disagreed about the enforcement of rules.

At Edgewood Cemetery the rules had said that the trustees could remove anything that was improper. Balloons, pinwheels, and statues were allowed at first, but they got out of hand, offending some people, says Snow. The rules were rewritten with specific restrictions. "Things get to look tacky. But obviously you have to be careful of what you say. They think it looks great," he says.

The corporate cemetery must live by rules, but the trustees of a small cemetery know that every life is an exception to the rules. Al Ryder knows that he's on the spot as an elected arbiter of good taste, but with an average of eight burials a year, he will be lenient. Ryder has lived in Mont Vernon for nearly forty years (but still doesn't consider himself an old-timer). He's looking after his friends and neighbors in the cemetery.

As we leave the cemetery, once more we are near the grave of the teenager killed in the car accident. That grave also has decorations that violate the rules. "I haven't gone over to look at it and I don't intend to," he says. He knows that grave is visited almost daily.

We pass some of the more recent burials where the family has marked the grave with a natural stone. "I will do the same when my time comes," Ryder says. He will use one of the stones he had to move out of his hayfield one summer.

The newest cemetery in our town is around the corner from our house. We used to call it the "empty cemetery" when giving visitors directions to our house, but a few years ago I realized that we no longer said that. The cemetery is filling up, and it is a difficult place to visit. We know many of these people. We step gingerly around the empty places in the family plots that await our living friends. This isn't a walk through history and old family names as in the old graveyards.

We know two women who have had to bury their sons here. Each woman had a bench put in by the grave. Driving by, I have seen, out of the corner of my eye, one of these mothers sitting by her son. It stops my breath.

It made her feel good to visit her son, one of them told me.

Her son had taught Latin in poor city neighborhoods. He was much loved. She often finds that others have been there and left flowers or stones on his grave in the Jewish custom, or other remembrances. This was a strong comfort, she said.

One family friend used to stop at her son's grave every Sunday on the way home from Mass. He was a retired diplomat, a tall man who dressed elegantly for church. He still wore a hat, and a long town coat. Even in winter, when the snow had drifted over the stone wall, he would troop right over to the grave. She remembers seeing his footprints in the snow. This is what we do for each other. It's the most we can do and sometimes the only thing. Small, solitary acts of homage. They are sometimes seen. They are communal.

II | Flaneurs

The
Flaneur | of the
Strip

The strip of stores and offices leading into the old mill city of Nashua, New Hampshire, from the northwest is seven and a half miles long with two dozen traffic lights, and an uncountable number of Dunkin' Donuts. It's not that the donut shops are as infinite as the heavens; it's just that each time I try to count them I lose track. The strip scrolls past the windshield like those cartoon backgrounds when the cat is chasing the mouse—the same four or five buildings repeating. Dunkin' Donuts, Mobil gas station, Market Basket supermarket, a four-story office building, a string of little shops with their signs pinned like nametags on a low, dun-colored building. It's difficult to remember where anything is on the strip. It's a post-landmark landscape. Anywhere, Everywhere, U.S.A. The Nashua strip is not postcard New England.

The strip runs from Route 101, the state's major east-west road, to Route 3, the choked interstate that heads to Boston and the high tech companies on the ring road. The strip is a commuter's gauntlet, an obstacle course. But tonight I am not trying to get *through* the strip, instead I have come to tour. My guide and driver is Dan Scully, an architect who understands the automobile better than anyone I know. While a student at Yale in the late 1960s, Scully was a part of the studio that went to Las Vegas to study the strip. He uses automobile imagery in some of his buildings. His house looks like a car: large piston and connecting-rod columns flank his garage. He has built a small classical pavilion, approached by a proper *allee.* It's a noble temple. Open the door, and there's a dragster charging at you. The dragster is a woodstove. "If Ferraris look fast just standing still, why not architecture as well?" Scully has written. Most of his clients prefer not to mix house and car, but I have seen him work two-lane blacktop into otherwise domestic scenes. (A roof crowned with a ten-foot-long Miss 1948 Desoto hood ornament; a hallway with a six-foot-tall piston and connecting rod.) After his house was published in the *New York Times,* no one called to have him design a house/car for them. (He calls it "carchitecture.") But *Ripley's Believe-It-Or-Not* took notice. This was not the attention he sought—*Ripley's* is a long way from the *Architectural Record*—but good naturedly he had a few t-shirts of *Ripley's* made and for awhile we called him the Believe-It-Or-Not Architect.

Scully loves cars, and races a 1959 Volvo on the weekends, but he also knows that cars destroy towns and cities. "Aren't we all just slaves to this motorized wheelchair?" he asks. "Merc-o-matic, Ultramatic, Cruise-o-matic, Dynaflow, Duoglide, Hydramatic, Fluidmaster, Flushomatic, Electro-touch-push-button-drive, Power Flite, Velva-touch . . . for your convenience," he once wrote. "God, I love 'em, but in being better than life, are these trade names . . . a sign of our removal, if not alienation, from the fluctuations of our natural environment?" He started his career with a group of idealistic solar architects determined to save America. They called their company Total Environmental Action, and they aimed for nothing less.

I have visited his buildings over the years, and I have seen these two impulses in his work: Hot Rod Scully and Good

Citizen Scully—the rebel Scully whose buildings challenge and upset people, and the proper Yankee whose buildings are discreet. The rebel built his house, a school in the shape of a train, and a lakeside summer cottage of corrugated metal and logs, which looks, he says, like a Lincoln Log set that has been kicked, the usual rectangle twisted to a parallelogram. Citizen Scully designed a perfectly nuanced restoration of a nineteenth-century Main Street store, replacing a tan metal Woolworth front with red-brick in step with its neighbors. Only two touches—an inward curving glass front, and a jaunty metal arch—reveal the rebel Scully, just as citizen Scully can be found in his train-shaped school. That school, an addition, thriftily incorporated two older buildings, and benefited from his solar design.

Like all the architects I know, he has a visceral reaction to bad architecture. It's painful. (Think of life as a daily, grade-school piano recital.) As we drive down the strip, he looks left at a pool and patio store highlighted in oranges and pool-blue, and turns away quickly. "A cartoon," he says in a grumbling voice. "A lot of these are just trying so damn hard for attention. They become cartoons of buildings. It's hard to do a restrained, refined building on the strip. It's all about competing for visual attention. It's all the same; it's all just wildly out of control. It's all bright. The communication is so frenetic, chaotic. *Everybody is yelling and screaming.*"

Scully has defined the principal experience of the strip: we enter a cartoon, we lose dimension. We are cartoon consumers, our legs windmilling in the chase as we repeat: we gotta have. The commercial strip and the cartoon strip are one.

I can be the happiest guy on earth, but by the time I am two or three stoplights into the Nashua strip, I'm sour. I'm an angry Puritan spoiling for a pulpit or a polemic. *The Day of Doom:* "We never looked for such days in New-England . . . [Are] all your promises forgotten?" It is a "damp, drizzly November in my soul" (to borrow Melville's phrase). This is not Thoreau's "New Hampshire everlasting and unfallen" that I love.

When I was growing up, the first "strip" I knew was Jericho

Turnpike on Long Island, which was in a gap-toothed adolescence. (One day there will likely be names for the phases of strip development.) Jericho Turnpike in the 1960s still had a few farms. It had sandy pits where "Will Build to Suit" signs and "Coming Soon!" signs stood long enough to weather and fade. This was the era of miniature golf, driving and batting ranges with their big black nets, and drive-in movies. (I remember John Wayne in all his tinny-speaker glory.)

Jericho wasn't the only strip. There were many others. It all blurred together. We had no name for it. There were the stores you shopped at, and other stores that were identical where you didn't shop.

As I grew up, all the sandlots and farms were built on as promised. The land became too valuable for drive-in movies and batting ranges. Strips of little stores became malls and big-box warehouse stores. Jericho strained at its four-lane limit, and the traffic engineers squeezed in turn lanes where they could.

Long Island churned up field after field for stores. I hated it. I thought this was only happening on Long Island. When I began to travel, I saw the same auto-maimed landscape in Upstate New York, Tennessee, New Jersey, and around the world. (How are you going to keep them on the Miracle Mile once they've seen the mall in the Yucatán?) The strip is the true International Style.

I have seen the birth of new strips again and again. In the early 1990s I drove across North Carolina from the Smokies to the flat, tobacco-growing Piedmont. North Carolina was booming. I saw the red earth peeled back for new shopping centers, roads, and gas stations with their tall signs like sunflowers facing the interstate. North Carolina looked like it was swallowing the Northeast whole. Here, once more, was Long Island, New Jersey, Florida . . . but new and ready for a go at the same old schemes. Pitch your tent, pave a meadow, and try to cash in. If it doesn't work, you move on.

I knew that I was getting close to a town when I saw the new Wal-Mart. They were built at the farthest reach of the town's strip and acted like a black hole of commerce. Many stores on the strip were faltering or abandoned. Finally I would arrive at the husk of a town. No one around, empty stores.

In New Jersey we lived for several years near Route 22. Daily we drove past the Leaning Tower of Pizza, the Big Bowling Pin (with a face and a hat), the ship-shaped furniture store, the big paint cans, the Giant Man sign of the lumber yard, and the blue-steel teepee. (Or lawn dart—it was open to interpretation. Being named the Ivory Tower Motel didn't clarify anything.)

We are but a thought in the mind of Route 22, we'd say. It can be oppressive living in a cartoon.

This is one-line architecture. Once you have seen it, you stop seeing it. These are not buildings that grow up with you, buildings in which you are seeing new things all the time. A good building is like a good book; rereading reveals richness. (If, as Vladimir Nabokov said, the only reading is rereading, then we should discount architecture reviews of new buildings and demand follow-up visits.)

In winter twilight or a summer morning, roadside buildings are unchanged. Roadside buildings don't live in conversation with other buildings. They are not actors in the ensemble of Main Street or a public square. They lack the drama of being seen across a common, on a hill, or glimpsed suddenly on a narrow side street. This is a slide show, the same scene over and over. (Or the same two scenes. The Leaning Tower of Pizza had jazzy red neon and disappointing pizza. The Bowling Pin wore a red hat at Christmas.)

On days when you thought the Republic was rotted to the sills, these buildings stepped forward as exhibits. They weren't boisterous, freewheeling, witty, or ironic. They were ugly; they were a dead end.

I hate the strip. Why? Here's my shopping list of despair:
1. No place of grace.
2. No value beyond the marketplace. No civic order.
3. The individual—first and last.

4. Any chance encounter is bad, i.e., "an accident."
5. No walking allowed. Here's a diagram of stupidity: I had to go to Sears, to a bookstore, and a computer store. The stores were at the same corner, just a couple hundred feet apart—but across an intersection of four-lane roads. There was no walking. Each time I exited a store I had to recross the intersection. A good part of our national wealth is tied up waiting for the light to change, all the shining cars with their ticking loans polluting the air and water.
6. On the strip I'm a consumer and nothing more. I consume cars, gas, food, computers. I consume the earth. I am appetite. I am anxious about time, about having and getting.
7. "Things are in the saddle and ride mankind." (Emerson)
8. If this is freedom, why is it tyranny?

Here's the answer to number eight. Philip Slater answered my question in his incisive book, *The Pursuit of Loneliness* (1970). Slater lists three "desires that are deeply and uniquely frustrated by American culture:

1. The desire for *community*—the wish to live in trust and fraternal cooperation . . .
2. The desire for *engagement*—the wish to come directly to grips with social and interpersonal problems . . .
3. The desire for *dependence*—the wish to share responsibility for the control of one's impulses and the direction of one's life."

On the strip we meet our desires and frustrations. We succeed as a marketplace and fail all other measures of democracy and civic sanity. The strip is a mirror, a snapshot. The strip is us. (And I still hate it.)

I am touring the strip with Scully to try and get beyond that hate. Hate is beside the point. We must ask: What's going on here? What have we authored? I'd rather be a flaneur of the strip than be Cotton Mather at the wheel, preaching to the dashboard.

In nineteenth-century Paris, the flaneur strolled the city at leisure studying the crowds. The flaneur was not a tourist; he was not interested in the guidebook's anecdotes and dates. "These are all so much junk to the flaneur, who is happy to leave them to the tourist," wrote Walter Benjamin. For Benjamin, a Weimar Germany intellectual, the flaneur was an important figure. The city was theater for the flaneur; the crowd was the show. Crowds were new; they were the harbinger of modern times. "To endow this crowd with a soul is the very special purpose of the flaneur," wrote Benjamin. "The flaneur is the priest of the genius loci. This unassuming passer-by with his clerical dignity, his detective's intuition, and his omniscience, is not unlike Chesterton's Father Brown, that master detective." The flaneur was not a sightseer, but rather a seeker of the spirit of the age, the *zeitgeist*.

On the strip the flaneur is no longer on foot. He cruises instead of strolls, but he is in the right place. The nineteenth-century flaneur welcomed crowds, while others feared them. The flaneur experienced the city as a landscape — "It becomes a landscape that opens up to him and a parlor that encloses him," wrote Benjamin.

The flaneur of the strip is not here to turn out the usual editorial against sprawl (it's bad) or to denounce America as the fallen landscape of ugly greed. (It's not Tuscany.) The flaneur is here to understand this new city.

"America is a fast, hard, and restless place carved out of the wilderness, where the European notion of social places as a fixed piazza has been redefined into moving along Main Street," Scully has written in a Japanese architecture magazine. "Cruising Main Street is the American notion of 'place.'"

When Dan Scully went to Las Vegas with the architects Robert Venturi, Denise Scott Brown, and Steven Izenour in 1969, they looked at the strip without rancor or scorn. (The Las Vegas Strip Beautification Committee seemed to have been bracing itself for a good New England scolding.) They were flaneurs in this new playscape for the masses.

"The Las Vegas strip eludes our concepts of urban form and

space, ancient or modern," reported *Learning from Las Vegas*. Vegas was not the broad boulevards of Haussman's Paris, Frank Lloyd Wright's suburban Broadacre City, or the early twentieth century Garden City. "It is something else again. But what? Not chaos, but a new spatial order relating the automobile and highway communication in an architecture which abandons pure form in favor of mixed media. . . . We term it sprawl, because it is a new pattern we have not yet understood."

On the Vegas strip "the sign is more important than the architecture . . . If you take the signs away, there is no place." The book's photos record now-vanished signs, like the classical pediment and columns of Caesars Palace advertising Jack Benny, Flip Wilson, and Petula Clark (in different shows). The Vegas signs were spectacular; they are the aspiration of every roadside business and the bane of all zoning boards.

(Coincidentally, the flaneur became, in his last transformation, a paid stroller wearing an advertising signboard, a "sandwichman," said Benjamin.)

Learning from Las Vegas (1972) is an intelligent, calm book that is worth reading thirty years later. It may have been the first time that the suburban, postwar landscape was written about without anger. The usual approach to the American landscape was a full-tilt screed. Peter Blake's *God's Own Junkyard* (1964) is the classic polemic "written in fury," as he said. "In America today, no citizen (except for an occasional hermit) has a chance to see anything but hideousness—all around him, day in and day out," Blake wrote. "Our suburbs are interminable wastelands dotted with millions of monotonous little houses on monotonous little lots and crisscrossed by highways lined with billboards, jazzed-up diners, used-car lots, drive-in movies, beflagged gas stations, and garish motels. Even the relatively unspoiled countryside beyond these suburban fringes has begun to sprout more telephone poles than trees, more trailer camps than national parks. . . .

"Why have we permitted this outrage? Why do we continue to permit it?"

God's Own Junkyard contrasted the "hideous scars" and "festering sores" of America-the-mutilated with approved good taste in 157 black-and-white photos: Thomas Jefferson's great lawn at the University of Virginia is pitted against the signs and wires of Canal Street in New Orleans; Beacon Hill in Boston stared down Salt Lake City; a tree-lined country lane is contrasted with the litter along a road of gas stations and powerlines; and aerial photos of rows of new suburban houses are matched with piles of junked cars and gravestones. All the good taste was upper class; blight was middle class. Unfortunately, the author trips in the bramble of his own snobbery. Blake is right; the new model America circa 1960 is ugly, but his attack is part of the high-minded tut-tutting of his era, the good-taste police revulsed once more by the masses.

We drive the strip after rush hour when the night-paving crews are at work under the dramatic NASA launchpad lighting. (It looks like a W.P.A. mural of workers. Heroic.) There is construction all along the road. We read a sign: 136,000 square feet for lease. "That's done entirely on spec," says Scully. "I'll tell you, that's gutsy. If you drive up and down here, half of it's empty." Indeed, many of the faux Colonial villages are dim. (The conceit: We're really not a shopping center, just old houses that have bumped into each other.)

I had thought that the Nashua strip was all built up. It's hell to drive through. But as a chauffeured flaneur at leisure, for the first time I see the gap-toothed pattern I remember from my childhood near Jericho Turnpike. There's a driving range with black nets, antique stores in old sheds, a sign offering eighteen acres for sale. We drive past buildings that have been torn down. "What was there?" We can't remember. We're in a cartoon. We pass the expected fast food franchises, the 7-11's and their competitors (also uncountable). "What percentage of all this food is fried?" Scully asks. (Fifty-seven percent of Americans eat at least one meal a day outside the home. This is our national health plan.) For evenings there are the upscale, get-a-baby-sitter-we're-dining-out franchises, like the pizza place in terra-cotta colors with Tuscan red awnings. "Definitely a trip to Italy," he says. "A lot of them are just bright lights in space."

The strip ends with a rat-a-tat-tat of gas stations just before the interstate. The cloverleaf is just about the only open green space we've seen. "If they could figure out how to get commercial action there they'd probably do it," Scully says. Beyond the cloverleaf Nashua's downtown neighborhoods start. We turn around.

Heading back we stop at the new Home Depot, which is built on a hill over the strip. They had to blast out tons of rock. "They were willing to take on a horrendously expensive piece of land to develop. Huge site development costs. And that's a big thing with all these people: site development costs," he says.

Where I remember there once was a small farmhouse, we turn and enter a deep stone cut, the kind of thing you see along the Interstate. "I feel like I'm going into a tomb. Remember Mycenae where you go through the rock wall to the end of the cave?" Scully asks, referring to the beehive-shaped tombs that were cut into the limestone hills of Greece around the fourteenth century B.C. We're on a private parkway, winding up the hill. "We're going to another world here. They're not going to let us shop at anything else here." Up top is the brown and orange warehouse store.

"This is an Acropolis," Scully says.

"Home Depot Acropolis," I say, trying it on.

"But the parking lot is the monument," he says. From the lot we can see miles into the countryside. The parking lot lights must blight the night sky.

He scans the facade. "Now what right do they have—'Home Depot: New Hampshire's Home Improvement Warehouse.' Wait a minute: I saw one of those in Massachusetts. I saw one in Connecticut—What do you mean New Hampshire's? The money's going out of New Hampshire."

"It's like you once said about the Applebee's sign that says, 'Neighborhood Grill & Bar.' It's not your neighborhood bar," I say. "It's not like you know the family. You come in and they look at your new baby, or go out to the curb to look at your new car. You've seen that family through bad times and good. You pretty much know the gossip about the family, the crazy brother and the strange aunts. Even though the food has fallen off, you keep eating there because it's the neighborhood place. That's not what's going on at Applebee's. At your neighborhood bar the food stinks and you still go because you have a loyalty to the family. On the strip they could bulldoze the joint minutes after you've paid the bill and walked out the door and you might never notice. What was there?"

We stop for dinner at a pit of nostalgia, the Time-Less Diner. A restaurant in earth tones (brown clapboards and the word "Green" in the name) has been remade into a 1950s stainless steel diner. The place glitters. Inside they've poured on the (re-production) "memories": a Rock-Ola Juke Box (playing CDs), pedal cars hanging from the ceiling, the front of a '57 Chevy mounted like a deer head on the wall, gas pumps, James Dean pictures, boomerang squiggles on the Formica table, a traffic light, a barber pole, a Mobil sign, colorful neon on a malt machine, black and white floor tiles, and the waitresses dressed in a bobby-soxer motif.

"It's cute," say three women as they leave.

On the menu I order a souvlaki with their "famous" sauce. How can it be famous? They have only been open a few months.

In the thirty years since the Yalies went to the desert to study Las Vegas, America has lined thousands of miles of roads with fast food and malls. I read Scully a line from *Learning from Las Vegas:* "We term it sprawl, because it is a new pattern we have not yet understood." Is that still true? I ask.

No. It's a predictable pattern by now, he answers. Most of these strips started small, a hot dog stand, a corner of the family farm sold for a few house lots. "And it just starts to slowly disintegrate," he says. "You can't see it while it's happening— 'Oh, we'll build a house and it won't change anything.' And all of a sudden it's all changed. The forces keep pushing for more land and bigger signs. They go to the planning board and say we've gotta have a sign this big. Who says you gotta have? We're so big we get whatever we think we want. Gotta have.

You never know, do they really have statistics behind them that say nobody will buy if the sign is less than fourteen feet deep? Christ, they get a sign, they get a building that's orange. They got so much damn signage going on they could build it without the sign."

The pattern is known. We have sprawl's rap sheet. For more than a half century, the strip has been a big part of American life. "Thousands of people drive through here daily. The Wal-Mart parking lot is jammed at 9 P.M.," I say. "And yet no one puts this on a postcard: 'Hey, I'm living in New Hampshire.' It looks the same as any place else."

"Is there a comfort in that?" Scully asks. "There must be."

Comfort. Cartoons are comforting. No one is really hurt when the mouse dynamites the cat. The strip is marketed with the come-on of comfort (the Comfort Inn) and with the promise of a home on the road, a home where nobody knows your name and they're glad to see you as long as you can pay. The strip lives in the contradiction of the name Home Depot—domesticity on a gargantuan scale. Home—"a person's native place," "at ease," "deep; to the heart," says the dictionary, and Depot, "a storehouse or a 'warehouse.'" (Warehouse of the Heart?)

In the post-World War II boom, these contradictions troubled many Americans. The popular press and best-seller lists fretted over this affluent, mass consumer society. Books like *The Split Level Trap* tore into suburbia. *The Lonely Crowd, The Organization Man,* and *Life in the Crystal Palace* worried about a culture dominated by large corporations. In a telling phrase, sociologist David Riesman called this new landscape "the suburban dislocation." Who had the map to this new America?

In that era John Cheever, an elegant writer whose stories were mapping one kind of upscale suburb, wrote a short list: "A Miscellany of Characters That Will Not Appear." Number three was:

"All scornful descriptions of American landscapes with ruined tenements, automobile dumps, polluted rivers, jerry-built ranch houses, abandoned miniature golf links, cinder deserts, ugly hoardings, unsightly oil derricks, diseased elm trees, eroded farmlands, gaudy and fanciful gas stations, unclean motels, candlelit tearooms, and streams paved with beer cans, for these are not, as they might seem to be, the ruins of our civilization but are the temporary encampments and outposts of the civilization that we—you and I—shall build."

The "scornful descriptions" have receded. We seldom complain about this landscape anymore. Now and then a community makes a brave stand against a Wal-Mart or a Rite Aid. They are portrayed as adherents of the Flat Earth. (Stop commerce? You might as well repeal gravity.) But mostly we don't look at the strip. We lack the fresh inquiry of *Learning from Las Vegas,* the anger of *God's Own Junkyard,* or John Cheever's hope. I'd like to sign up with Cheever, but I'm afraid that this "temporary encampment" is our civilization. Coming Soon! More of the same.

The Bottom
of the Lake

At lunch one humid July afternoon I set out to tour a lake that vanished 10,000 years ago. Twenty-three thousand people live on this lake bottom today, in a city called Keene, unaware that this settlement is founded on catastrophe, as are all settlements. Catastrophes—sudden floods, earthquakes, landslides, millions of years of uplift and erosion—are common talk for geologists. In the sweep of a phrase they move mountains and rivers, send continents crashing into one another, and reverse the poles. Theirs is a science of unsettlement. And yet we choose to build here, because, well, where else is there?

My guide is Jeff Porter, a "planner by accident" and a naturalist by heart and training. Porter is rail-thin, with graying blond hair tied in a pony tail, a mustache, and goatee. He speaks with an economy learned from thousands of hours of late-night planning board meetings, but when he gets to talk geology, he's like a horse loosed from the barn. The same economy of speech takes on a quickened intensity. He grew up in Pennsylvania fishing and hunting and knocking around the woods with his hillbilly neighbors. His early heroes were Beatrix Potter, Marlin Perkins, and Jane Goodall. For his graduate studies he lived for a year with a flock of Canada geese, noting their movements all day into a tape recorder: "Head up. Head down. Head up. Head down," he repeats trance-like. He would sit in his tent all night transcribing the tape. "It was nonsense. Way overkill."

We get in his little Subaru Justy, a car that could fit in a drink holder of an SUV. He uses it like a Swiss Army knife—canoe on the roof, mountain bikes on back, gear for fishing and softball packed inside.

We start at Central Square, the common at the head of Main Street, but right away the bottom falls out and the sky is covered over. The lake was thirty feet deep here. We are underwater. But that was the lake's depth in its last years as sand, clay, and silt collected on the bottom. When they drove pilings for a city parking garage a few years back they had to dig through eighty feet of sand to hit bedrock. So take away eighty feet beneath the little red Subaru—water eight stories below us—and remember that there is water three stories above us. We are submerged, a little red submarine with the windows opened to the July heat. Everyone else waiting at the light assumes that they are on solid ground. We know better.

The lake was small compared to the glacier that preceded it. "It's enticing to look at the face of the mountain glaciers that we have today or even the bigger glaciers in Antarctica, look at the front of one of those, and say that must be what it was like here twelve thousand years ago. But I think that the magnitude, the scale was so much *greater*," Porter says, his voice a whisper. "*Just so immense.* You've probably seen drawings of the extent of the Laurentide Glaciation. *God!* the ice was almost two thousand meters thick here."

"Right here—ice more than a mile thick?" I ask. We're stopped at a light at the foot of Main Street.

"*Yeah.* You can't hardly imagine it."

Our text for this trip is Genesis, but the story is told in maps. Before we set out I met Porter at his office at the Southwest Region Planning Commission, where he is the assistant director. We sat down in a conference room. He talked me through a series of maps, placing one on top of another, until there were seven maps on the table, fanning out like a hand of cards.

The first map looked like a mustard stain with blue veins. (I took his word that it was a map. There was no topography or coordinates.) The yellow showed the stratified drift deposit, the sand and gravel left behind by running water from the melting glacier. Good places to find ground water. The dark and lighter blue veins marked the 500 foot and 480 foot elevations. Taken together, stains and veins, this was the silhouette of two ancient lakes, Lake Ashuelot, where Keene is today, and the much larger Lake Hitchcock, today's Connecticut River Valley.

He dealt the next map, moving from silhouette to a full portrait—a topographical map with the outlines of Lake Ashuelot over Keene. A nearly perfect fit; the city sat where the lake once was. We returned to the mustard stains with the next map—traditional yellow and a darker tan mustard, another view of where the lake may have been. The yellow was sand, and the tan was clay and silt. The tan showed the still waters at the middle of the lake, surrounded, north and south, by sand. The sandy areas may have had a more volatile history, being at different times lake and river delta—a river that may have been dammed.

Porter dealt his last card, a city street map on which he had highlighted the outlines of the lake and where we would visit that day. His finger picked out parks, schools, and cemeteries as he spoke of lake shore, river deltas, and a possible catastrophic event creating an Alluvial Fan—a torrent of water and earth.

Our first stop is the Branch River, where a large stone arch bridge had once carried the railroad. Up a short steep hill from the river and the road is the ancient lake shore. In twelve thousand years the now-modest Branch River had worked its way down from the level hilltop through forty or fifty feet of glacial till. It was still working, cutting down through the till. We stood where the river had entered the lake, creating a delta.

Porter points to the oaks and pines on the hill. "A mixed hardwood forest community seems pretty happy out here, which leads me to believe that this isn't a homogenous deposit," he says. Something dramatic may have happened here. A river flowing into a lake over thousands of years leaves layers of fine sand. We would be looking at sand-loving pine trees.

He sets the scene: The post-glacial landscape was barren. Yards of loose, unsorted material on the uplands were worn away by torrential run-off for thousands of years. "There's a neat feature called an Alluvial Fan. It happens in mountainous regions still where they'll be an upland lake that's created by a natural impoundment—maybe an avalanche created it at some point. The dam gives way and several billion gallons of water roar down a mountainside and carry everything in its path. Everything goes and gets dumped—wham—when it hits wherever the bottom is. An Alluvial Fan is catastrophic." Instant delta.

He's speculating, he adds cautiously. And then, as if he had not moved enough earth with one description, he points to other parts of the Branch River Delta that might have been created on top of the glacier.

I must confess to having a static view of the frozen world. In my mind the glacier rolls down from Hudson Bay and rolls back up like a window shade. I think this comes from encyclopedia diagrams and their chief fiction that the world is orderly and explainable in one short entry. In the encyclopedia the Ice Age is as mundane as a railroad schedule.

The glacier rolls up leaving lakes and rocks and sand. Not quite. "These glaciers were also melting downward at the same time. Glaciers had a whole topography on top that got laid on the earth's surface." They had another topography underneath. Lakes can be forming beneath a glacier. When the glacier leaves, the earth's crust rebounds and that lake becomes like a milk shake. "It's called liquefaction. It's when there's a suspension of soil particles in the water." All of this shows up as stratified drift deposits on those mustard maps.

"In twelve thousand years there are so many variables," Porter says. He adds others: these river deltas moved through the millennia; the continental crust rose, relieved of the glacier's weight—in the Northeast, three-and-a-half millimeters a year. After that, gravity pulls down the glacial features, and we come along with the ax and the bulldozer, rearranging the land in three hundred short years.

The glacier's exit was dramatic. "Just imagine the snow melt we have after a good winter," Porter says. "Multiply that by hundreds. You know we get three feet of snow left in the woods in April and we think: boy it's really roaring. Amplify that by hundreds of times and make it last for two thousand years." A two-thousand-year-long mud season.

So much for the encyclopedia's glacier, draped like a white sheet over North America. The Abenaki have it right in their story of how the giant Odzihozo carves out a lake, Bitownbauk. Odzihozo stands up, pushing the earth aside to make mountains. Years go by and water rushes in where he sat. The Abenaki have been telling this story since the glacier receded more than ten thousand years ago. We call this long narrow lake, Champlain. The glacier created our land.

When prospecting for signs of the glacier, look for gravel pits, airports, housing developments, and cemeteries, Porter says. (Level, well-drained soil.) Searching for Lake Ashuelot we make our way from St. Joseph's Cemetery to Woodland Cemetery, skirting North Cemetery, and Monadnock View Cemetery. The deep past is buried in graveyards.

Pan-flat St. Joseph's Cemetery sits on a small rise just south of the downtown. It's the top of the delta. This was lake level for a long period. Driving up a small hill, over the Branch River, one drives out of the lake.

On the map of the two mustards, this area was tan. The lake was calm just below the cemetery, allowing fine clay to settle. This is known as varved clay, layers of fine winter sediments and coarser spring sand that can be dated like tree rings. From this clay, Hampshire Pottery made its highly-valued Arts and Crafts vases and bowls. (Antiques made from antiquity.) Hampshire Pottery (1871 to 1923) is remembered by a historical marker just downhill from St. Joseph's.

We are near the southern end of the lake, where archeologists have found some of the places the Indians lived as long as 10,500 years ago, not far from the glacier's retreat in a barren landscape. There may have still been ice here.

We cross the city heading for our next cemetery by following the lake shore on Eastern Avenue. The street sits on a hill left by the glacier. "The till accumulated at the foot of the slope against the ice, and then when the valley filled up with water—lap, lap, lap—waves eroded it, cut it away, cut it away, created a bank," he says. There are quite a few elderly in this neighborhood sitting on lawn chairs facing the absent lake, as if somehow they knew.

The dead in Woodland Cemetery are resting in a different part of the lake. "Plainly down at the bottom here, nice and wet. Look at the pine trees. We're on sand and silt," he says.

Woodland is a big cemetery with a swamp at its center. Porter has ridden six miles in here on his bicycle.

"You have to wonder: well, a couple of things could have happened here. One is: this is just all that ever got deposited. Or two: this was all filled in and got eroded out again. Originally this might have been a deep hole in the lake."

We are sitting on a road by the chapel looking across the swamp to the other side of the cemetery, looking at land much the way the lake left it. The land falls off steeply by the road. "Look at this bank. Lake shore. Cool. Should have a fishing pole." I look over, surprised by the sharp drop.

"I knocked myself out riding my bike down that hill once."

"You did? You hit something?"

"A lot of things, I guess. I don't really remember. Started out okay."

"Mountain bike?"

"Yeah."

Porter wants me to see Lake Ashuelot up close. "The best way to appreciate post-glacial geomorphology is by mountain bike, horseback, or foot," he says. "Moving around in cars, the grades on the roads and the speed at which you move obliterate an awful lot of interesting gradations."

We walk for a few minutes back into the pine forest by the Jonathan Daniels Elementary School and talk of fishing. Around here he catches a limited menu of fish. Back where he grew up in Pennsylvania the fishing (and forests and geology) was more varied.

He scrambles down a slope. "Check that out. Is that incredible or what?" he says, pointing to where a woodchuck has been digging in the pine needles. There's a fine powdery silt. "That's what this is made out of. Isn't that amazing? This is right at the edge of the lake, which makes me think this was the waterfront."

As a river meets a lake, "fine sand and silt are the last things to fall out. And here it is. But if you just go back a little bit—" He scrambles back uphill. Porter moves fast, and I follow, sweating in the heat. He stops at a square pit (a signature digging of teenage boys, I think). The first time I found this, I was afraid that I might find bones, he says. But look: coarse sand with pebbles. The sand washed out as the river slowed. The coarser sand fell out here by this pit, and the finer silt down the slope as the river entered the lake. We can't step in the same river twice, or even once in a departed river, but here I have a handful of sand moved by the waters of a melting glacier.

Twelve thousand years ago this was a swamp at the edge of a lake stretching a dozen miles south from where we stood now in a pine forest by an elementary school. "This was the real backwater of the lake. That was all mucky back here, all full of frogs and grass. All the leaves and vegetation got deposited there.

"Nice spot."

The shape of the lake is, largely, the shape of the city. Keene's doppelganger, its ghost partner, is the vanished lake.

We drive across the city noting when we enter and leave the

lake. (Underwater. Above water. Underwater.) Porter searches through layers of time, trying to sort out "twelve thousand years of gravity and weather and ecologies." The rivers snaking over the valley floor, the earth pressing back against the glacier, one chapter of Genesis laid over the next.

"There were such titanic forces at work," I say. "We've snuck in here and built this stuff in a relatively calm period."

"Very."

"And we think we've got it licked."

"Very much so. Glaciation's a beautiful thing."

We end our tour at the landfill. He pulls up to the small gatehouse where a woman is collecting dump fees. "Just sightseeing," he says. The woman shakes her head.

The landfill is now a transfer station. The "dump" is capped, a big grassy dome. The methane is piped off to generate electricity. Sheep graze on the hill. Walking up to the top, we agree that we wouldn't eat that mutton. (I haven't seen it on menus: Our own local Landfill Chops! Methane Mutton.) "My couch is here," he says.

The hill stinks from methane. Each footfall sends up a cloud of small grasshoppers. At the top is the best view of Keene's valley that I have ever seen. A few miles off, between the fold of the hills, I can see the spire of the First Church, which sits at the head of the square where we began our tour. This was a travel brochure view, the kind in which the city would be described as "nestling" in the hills. But after two hours of touring geological time, I look at Keene with the eyes of a burglar. The doors are wide open. On this summer's afternoon between glaciers, the city sits defenseless, moments from being swept away.

The Otter
Mates for Life

The world was a larger place when John Kulish was alive, and any day that you hiked with John in the woods was a bigger day. John was in his late seventies when I first knew him, an old woodsman who had fed his family in the Depression and after World War II by trapping bobcat, otter, beaver, fox, and mink. Long ago he had put away his traps. He knew animals in the wild as intimately as they can be known. "People say I'm a trapper. I'm not. I'm an animal psychologist. No one knows what I know," he said—actually he declaimed. John had lost much of his hearing. Struck by lightning at age six, he was silent until high school, when he managed to stutter. He had achieved his own pronunciation. (He said "my-in" for mine.) He was struck by lightning again in the Navy. He had volunteered right after Pearl Harbor. At his induction, the Navy doctors were shocked when they looked in his ears and flushed out a forest floor's worth of pine, spruce, and hemlock needles, twigs, leaves, and bark. "Where the hell have you been?" they asked him. He had been in the woods every possible moment he could, skipping school. He was learning to read animal sign, the stories animals leave with their tracks, scratchings, traces of fur or feathers, and most importantly their droppings, which naturalists call "scat." "I know scat like the American knows the almighty God," he declaimed once standing around a campfire. There were about a dozen of us warming by the fire, but his voice could have carried to the last row of a large theater. He opened his stories like Homer, ready to sing of great voyages. "I think I've lost my eyesight studying scat," he said. Without trying, John Kulish had a stage presence.

John led a few hikes each year for the Harris Center, the conservation foundation and nature sanctuary in our town. I went along whenever I could. They were unlike all other hikes on the Harris Center's calendar. The book-trained naturalists moved differently in the woods; they walked as if down an aisle in the supermarket. They were looking for things—very consciously looking—for animal sign, tree species, etc., calling on their education as if they were in Paris summoning their best French. John walked as if thousands of acres surrounded each step—which it did. In the woods John was quite like a bobcat or an otter: he belonged, he strode, he smiled, he knew where he was. When anyone else led a hike, you had a good time, and learned a few things, but John used up all the daylight and covered the countryside. We could hardly keep up with this senior citizen. Into his eighties he was spry and slightly built. He said he had never seen a big, burly man who had the endurance to keep going for hours in the woods. "Grit" is what mattered. Grit had kept John going when his feet were bloody, when he had to plunge into a river in near-zero temperatures, when it was getting dark and he was hungry, wet, and miles from home.

The woods of Stoddard, New Hampshire, were his university. Or as he often declaimed, "I spent fifty-five years in my university, the university without walls, Stoddard University." He wanted to know what made a deer a deer or an otter an otter. He wanted to know how they thought and how they felt.

Early in his education he had seen deer starve on a full stomach. In a hard winter, the mounting snow confines deer to their yard. They run out of the fresh buds they need, five to seven pounds a day, he said. So they eat pine needles and other things that have no nourishment. When he was fourteen years old he had cut open a dead deer's stomach and found this out. As deer starve, the bone marrow goes from red to white. This knowledge set him apart from young ecologists. John had blood on his hands; he had his hands in the viscera of life.

John dressed the same for the winter hikes no matter how cold it was. He wore a thin canvas jacket such as you might wear indoors in a drafty old house. No gloves, no scarf, sometimes a hat. I have seen him dressed this lightly on a February day when it was twelve degrees with a stiff wind. We were all wrapped up in our layers of polypropylene and wool, some of us looking a little like a balloon in the Macy's Thanksgiving Day parade. John stood among us, dressed for a spring thaw, a day in the forties.

In a small canvas backpack he carried a long-handled ax, which hung half-way to the ground, and the all-important number ten can. This heavy ax had but one job: to cut down one branch, a sapling, to hang the number ten can over the fire at lunch. And this fire had only one purpose: to boil water for tea. John placed the number ten can, with its small wire handle inches above the fire—it was blackened from hundreds of fires. He put about a dozen Red Rose tea bags in this and let it boil for maybe twenty minutes. Strongest damn tea you'll ever taste—a mix of wood-smoke and twigs and tin and tanin magnified. This tea had an attitude. After a cup, I was ready to start at a good clip for the moon. I can still see him standing a ways from the fire, drinking his tea and smiling broadly. He never sat down. He never ate lunch.

His magic tea would hold him past sunset. Winter days are short, and even shorter in the woods where the dark rises early. (Or as Yogi Berra once said, it gets late early out there.) I have been with him in the woods late as the bluish shadows grew and it would have been prudent to head for home, but John would add on a few miles, tag on a tour of two more highland lakes, or places he used to hunt bobcat.

There was no way to turn him around. One time we had snowshoed over Bald Mountain and had come to the trail that led back to where we had started. It was late, and many of us were tired. A day on snowshoes, the old wide ones, was like a day on a horse. This was before we had converted to the lighter metal and plastic snowshoes. John never surrendered the five-foot-long snowshoes he'd worn trapping and hunting.

Meade Cadot, the director of the Harris Center, pointed out the trail to John. Meade and John had a complicated relationship. John didn't like most college-educated naturalists, and that was that. John ignored him. Meade then made the mistake of taking out his compass and telling John the direction.

"I know where I am!" John shouted. He was angry at the sight of Meade's compass. It would be like offering a member of the Academie Française your Berlitz phrase book: *Parley-voo Fran-say?* John stalked off, cracking through the brush. He wanted to look for bobcat tracks, and this was the route bobcat traveled. He was really moving now.

Behind him the hike was in disarray. We trailed for a quarter mile. The hill was thick with pine branches—brittle the way they get once the needles are gone. Twenty-five of us smashed our way forward, the sound of dead pine boughs snapping off all over the hill—a group of five over here, six more there in the dim light. Napoleon's army in retreat from Moscow.

I had branches sticking out of my hair and my coat. I always wore a ripped up old winter coat for John's hikes. He didn't stay on trails; he ran into the brush like some animal wary of the open, as if a hawk might swoop in and take him. Otter, he said, would not cross a path if they picked up a human scent. John would come to a trail, decry snowmobiles, and bushwhack back in—even if the path ran parallel. In my clunky snowshoes it was all I could do to step around the trees and fallen logs. (John, in much longer snowshoes, had no trouble.)

He stayed on a trail only long enough to give his snowmobile speech. Years ago some snowmobilers had seen him hiking in the Pisgah wilderness:

"How'd you get here?"

"I walked."

"You walked? How old are you?"

"How old do you think I am?"

"Forty-five."

"I'm sixty-five."

"'Oh well, you know,' they said, 'we'd love to walk, but, but . . .'"

And with a triumphant smile John would plunge us all back into a thicket. It wasn't a hike unless there was a stick in your eye.

John had led us to the top of a bobcat ledge, a five or six story granite cliff covered in ice and snow. We went over the cliff. One after another we took off our snowshoes, held them to our chests, and lay down. We shot down an icy chute, banking off the different granite rocks, human pinballs.

The sun had set. My wife, worried, had begun calling around. I went home and floated my sore limbs in the bathtub. For John Kulish it was just another day in the woods.

The only time John stopped for long was to lecture. It was a set scenario, the aria in the opera. I knew it was coming; I'd heard it before. I dressed for it. I wore extra socks, long johns, more layers than I would otherwise. He had a tendency to hold forth out on a windswept, frozen pond. As he moved into his tenth minute you could feel the cold seeping up into you.

We would stop by an otter track. John would talk about otters and then ask if anyone knew why their tail was uniquely triangular. (To turn quickly like a fish.) Invariably, a young ecologist from the nearby college would answer—incorrectly. Always. I went on his winter hikes for years, and there was always a new volunteer with the wrong answer.

That ignited John: How can you learn about the outdoors if you're not outdoors? He was indignant. "I spent fifty-five years in my university, the university without walls, Stoddard

University," he would begin, and then rip into book-trained naturalists, the state's "know-nothing" fish and game officers, and worst of all, *Pee-H-Dee's*. He said that as if he were slashing a machete, each letter cutting a swath. He raised his voice above the usual shout: *Pee-H-Dee*. It was a swear word.

He had met a Pee-H-Dee in Vermont who said that coyote were feeding on deer carcasses. John said how could that be? This is deep snow here. Your dog is up to his snout—his nose is sticking up like a periscope. A coyote weighs the same. These tracks only sink in two inches. These are fox. Later the Pee-H-Dee identified beaver scat. No, said John, I've never known a beaver that could swim fast enough to catch a fish. There's fish bones in this scat. This is otter scat.

Onward the frozen lecture minutes ticked: "You can't learn that in books . . . He doesn't get out of his car and walk . . . He's been behind his desk too long . . . Fish and Game don't know . . . Some Pee-H-Dee says to me . . . Professors are pedantic fools. They know book stuff. But my library is out here, the laboratory without walls . . ."

I knew his lectures by heart. I didn't mind. The man was right. If you're going to be a naturalist, ecologist, environmentalist—call it what you will—but get your ass outdoors.

John killed his first wild animal at age nine. He trapped a rabbit. Heading home with his prize, he wondered what the rabbit's mother would say when her little rabbit never came home.

When he grew up, he worked summers in a factory at his parents' urging. In the 1920s you could make a steady living in New England's mills. John broke free for the woods. He worked long, hard days as a trapper, leaving home hours before daylight, and returning in darkness. There was never enough time. There were always more miles to hike, more traps to set. He never ate lunch, never sat down. He was always hungry. The basket of his backpack was seldom empty. He would run a line of steel traps and return home with a twenty-pound otter. He worked through the miseries of New England's winters. "A day that began with my snowshoes skimming over frozen crust could end up ankle-deep in water and thigh-deep in wet snow," he said. In the Great Depression winter of 1933, it never rose above zero all January.

His family—his wife, Aino, and their two daughters—lived "close to the bone." They had a root cellar of potatoes, beets, carrots, and cabbage, preserved wild berries, and a freezer full of hare, grouse, wild duck, horned pout, and deer. (Their daughter, Johanna, didn't like the hot school lunches; there was no venison.)

A trapper's wife had to be resourceful and have a good sense of humor, Aino said. She had to be "a woman who, when the larder is empty of staples, climbs into a shed loft, grabs a bushel basket brimming with porcupine heads, some ripening since October, and trundles them to the home of a selectman-judge, to collect the fifty cents per head bounty. A woman who, while chairmanning a PTA policy committee meeting, can ignore the sudden green faces of her colleagues when the piercing pungency of mink musk seeps up from the cellar where her trapper husband is skinning next week's groceries," Aino wrote with John in *Bobcats Before Breakfast.* The book is a woodsman's memoir, John's stories but not his voice. If it were written as he spoke, the book would be as strong as whiskey.

John wanted to title the book *Rubber Bottoms, Leather Tops,* in homage to the famous L. L. Bean boot that had kept him dry in wet snow, slush, and rain. He wore out two pair a year and got them resoled. A trapper's boots were as important as a scalpel was to a surgeon, he said. By tying the top tight with a rawhide lace, he had a watertight shoe to ford brooks and wade through bogs. Other than his boots, the tools he relied on were few: compass, shotgun, trail axe, and jackknife.

He trapped fox in the 1920s. Fox coats were the fashion. After the great stock market crash, in November 1929, fox pelts fell in price. He had been paid thirty-five dollars a pelt. Fox are hard to catch, and the trappers who could catch a hundred in two months never let on how they did it. If they found another trapper encroaching, they spit near their traps. That kept the fox away.

After John returned from the Navy, he hunted bobcat. Fox coats were out of fashion, and the local fox population was beset with mange. New Hampshire put a twenty dollar bounty on the cats. Hunting bobcat was "grueling and lonely." He could search for days in perfect snow conditions without seeing a track. He pursued the cats as they led him through the roughest parts of the country, the ledges, thickets, swamps, and tangled blow downs left by the devastating 1938 hurricane. Just one cat had led him on a five-day-long, fifty-mile chase. He had snowshoed 2,000 miles to learn bobcat behavior, he said.

He hunted bobcat with his hound dogs. Over the years he had trained and hunted with some forty hounds, but only two stood out, Tim and Jiggs, who was "the truest friend I had ever had." From the first, John saw Jiggs's "dignity." Jiggs was smart, discerning grey fox tracks from bobcat tracks, and he was brave, having survived a fight with a wounded bobcat and thirty cold hours trapped in a ten-foot-deep hole near the summit of Mount Monadnock. His wife had painted a portrait of Jiggs, which hung over the hearth in John's last house.

John was a student of all the animals he hunted. He watched beavers swimming under the ice exhale a bubble and then breathe it back in, something that had not been written about, he said. He frequently contradicted the conventional reports about animals, things people kept writing only because they had been written previously.

He loved otters above all. "Of all wild animals, the best minds, the best hearts," he said. They were God's favorite. God had been generous to otters, giving them love, he said. "The otter mates for life," John said. They had strong families. The male otter helped raise his pups and taught them with "firm kindness." They worked and played as families and never gave up playing. Otters were always on the go. John kept a census of the otters in a fifty-mile radius around his home, marveling at how they knew the shortest route between watersheds.

He would come upon them playing, diving and surfacing with an explosive flourish, snorting loudly, racing after each other in and out of the water in a game of tag. They never lost their sense of adventure, he said. He would like to be the kind of man an otter might be. John took a lesson from their play, and when feeling guilty about a stonewall to finish or a cellar to clean, he'd remember the otter and get his snowshoes or fishing pole. He had an otter's appetite—he loved brook trout and said that he would eat them every day if he could, heads and all.

John had an otter's playful spirit. He liked playing tricks. Once he was guiding some rich hunters who were nervous in the woods. It was deer season, and as he guided them, he taught them how to read deer scat. How recent was it? Was it a doe or a buck? He leaned in close to one pile and said "sometimes you have to pick it up." He grabbed a palm full. The hunters stood back. "Sometimes you have to smell it." He held it to his nose. The hunters were disgusted. "And sometimes you have to taste it." And with that John swallowed the deer scat. He had eaten raisins. He had walked ahead and planted them on the trail. You should have seen their faces, he said.

He played a trick or two on wildlife. In his canoe he could paddle right up to a moose. He paddled slowly, square on with the moose's nose. Moose, he said, have no depth perception. He'd reach out and pat the moose on the nose with his paddle. No one else did that; no one else would think of doing that.

Otters taught him another great lesson. From otters he learned that animals mourn. If you kill one otter, the other will stay nearby, "sometimes for many weeks, searching and waiting for its beloved." He had seen no other animals do this, he said. "The otter mates for life," he'd repeat. Tears came to his eyes when he said this.

The first time he trapped an otter, he was proud of his skill. But John was a good observer, and what he kept seeing troubled him. In the 1930s he had tracked a family of four otters. He caught the first three, an old male and two yearlings, and set out to find the fourth. At last he saw the surviving otter. She surfaced and watched the shore for nearly half an hour looking for her family. Then "she slowly slipped under the surface, leaving only a few gentle ripples." He had seen his first "forlorn otter." She was listless, no longer playful. For weeks the widow searched every cove of the pond "repeating her sad ritual as she grieved for her loved ones."

John continued to trap otter, but he was being hunted by the same question about mourning that had shadowed his first triumph as a nine-year-old trapper. Years later he trapped another otter family. He caught the first two, but the third was missing. He came upon the otter crying. "Whenever it surfaced, it let out a series of four or five throbbing, plaintive, almost dovelike sounds." He was watching a "gentle creature's breaking heart."

It had been more than forty years since he had witnessed that otter's suffering. It pained him still, and he told the story often on hikes. He wanted this lesson to stay with his listeners.

Too much death, too much suffering. He had to stop killing otter "more to end my own misery than theirs." His woods were changing. There were cottages now on many once-wild lakes. He gave up trapping. "The animals were good teachers. The otter were the best of all," he said. "Only by being an otter myself would I be able to understand more."

John never betrayed the tricks of his particular magicians guild. Other trappers offered him money to learn his tricks — money his family needed. He refused. When a game warden asked him how he knew where to set an otter trap, he answered, "I set it where the otter's going to put its foot."

Know-nothing naturalists weren't his only complaint. His family life had its sorrows. His youngest daughter, Heidi, had died from a brain tumor. He was estranged from his other daughter, and divorced. He was cramped by his anger at his surviving daughter. He would fall into that groove — he couldn't help himself. He would talk about something she had done when she was eleven or twelve years old, and he would start yelling like they used to, only now John also performed her part of the dialogue. On different evenings, over dinner, I had sat through three-hour-long monologues. The man had stamina. I would stare at the portrait of Jiggs. My wife would try to gently turn John to talking about anything else. As in the woods, you couldn't turn John around.

At home he could be a complaining, bitter man. These dinners were grim. Any day with an old man complaining—yelling in your direction—is a smaller day. You can feel the walls of the room closing in on you until they touch your shoulders.

John began a new career. He answered a want ad for a janitor at Boston University's camp in Peterborough, New Hampshire. It must have been a surprising interview. They put him right to work teaching. The environmental movement had created a generation eager to learn what he knew. When John was teaching he would "wake up whistling, and go to work whistling," he had told me. He gave those kids everything and led hikes through his old hunting grounds in Stoddard.

His university had a glorious, rough campus. The land was untamed: tight groups of rolling hills, huge granite boulders everywhere. From the 1820s to the 1850s, farmers had cleared this land for sheep pastures. Long ago it had grown back into forest. Hiking the tumble of the hills, you wondered at the notion of sheep farming: in some places there would have been more granite than grass.

We would cross the frozen North Branch River, hike up to the old Curtis graveyard and Holmes Hill, continue on around Nancy and Lightning Mountains, and head for home across Pioneer Pond, Pickerel Cove, and Highland Lake. (Unless John added a lake or two.)

The Curtis graveyard was miles from the nearest road. A stone wall defended a small rise. Two obelisks near the entrance marked the Curtis family plot. The last burial was about 1872. Pine and hemlock were crowding in behind the Curtis's, and far in the back was one lone gravestone for a woman, Eliza. When John had come across this graveyard many years ago there were more stones. Snowmobilers had gotten in and carted off some of the stones, he said. Someone had recently paid the dead some respect, cutting the small brush and trees in the plot.

On one winter's tour of the Stoddard highlands, it was early March after a light snow, and everyone was on the move. We saw a considerable amount of animal signs: Bear claw marks on a tree, a porcupine den, slides where two otters had played, a grouse's wingtip marks and nesting holes, the hide of a deer that had been picked clean by hungry coyote, and the tracks of snowshoe hare, weasel, and moose. The moose had browsed the tree trunks, slicing off thin strips of bark with their lower (and only) incisors, and then bedding down in the snow, leaving their improbably large imprints.

On another tour we had seen two otter slides, one just a few hours old. In the light snow of the morning, which sat on several inches of older snow, you could see each movement of the otter: how it pushed along with its front paws, where the rear feet were tucked in, how it had swished its tail. The individual hairs registered in the fine snow. We also saw moose browse, and the tracks of grouse, snowshoe hare, and maybe a coyote. But not much else. Everyone was holed up.

On this day John did not charge ahead. He walked about midway in the group. His lectures were shorter. He also fell twice on the ice, cutting his nose. Everyone rushed to his side, including several former students who had reunited just for this hike. His fall upset us. And when we resumed, we stepped lightly, as if testing a frozen lake to see if the ice would hold our weight.

John had a stroke at age eighty-four. He had many visitors at the hospital. My wife was already there sitting by his side when I walked in. John was telling a story. His speech was slurred, the recorder running on low batteries. His arm moved like puppet work. The words were unintelligible, but the cadence was familiar. He was in good spirits. My wife held his hand and asked occasional questions. I looked out the window: a cumulus cloud rose into view in the narrow window and then sailed across. Blue sky.

"The deer, a buck, I dropped him on the run," John said, the words snapping into clarity. These were the last words I heard him say. He died several days later.

John's memorial service was a nearly perfect remembrance in the garden at the Harris Center, under blue skies and puffy white clouds. He illuminated many lives. People stood up to share stories and brought forward objects: a stuffed otter, John's snowshoes, paddles, and his "old banjo." They had known John twenty-five, thirty-five, almost sixty years. They had canoed with him, eaten his hot spaghetti, trailed after him in the woods. They told what it was like to be with him when he paddled right under the nose of a moose to touch it with his paddle. They recalled how he had given up trapping otters.

When John was teaching he had told his students: Don't ever take a job just for the money. That's a hole you won't be able to dig out of. A few had listened, he said. And here they were, testifying to how John had changed their lives.

In his last years he worked outdoors maintaining the grounds of an estate. His co-workers spoke of how they loved to work with him, how diligently he worked. He chopped and stacked wood and said at the end, "There, that was a good job." He worked right until the end of his life and left all his money and his house — $115,000 — to the Harris Center. He requested that his ashes be spread behind his house with the ashes of his youngest daughter, Heidi, and his good friend Jiggs.

He would have loved the service: the dragonflies dancing about, the catbird calling, and he may have even liked what Meade Cadot said, "I'll look the next otter in the eye carefully. Could be John."

I miss John's stories. The old-timers literally knew these critters from the inside out, from trapping, gutting, and eating them. I enjoyed learning to distinguish the tracks of a least weasel from a mink. But I did not hike with him for the track-ing or woods lore. Around here you could swing a "fisha' cat" and knock over a dozen knowledgeable naturalists. I showed up for the freedom. In the woods John Kulish was that rarest animal, a free man. He was home.

III | Rpm

Boom

In the boom-boom-boom of New Hampshire's biggest boom, the talk was quicksilver, all boomtown boast, and boomtown worry about missing the Big Chance. You'd hear amazing stories: A man in Peterborough who had just bought his house was approached four times by people who told him, Let me know when you want to sell. I'll give you twenty thousand more. Call me. I'll give you forty thousand more. Here's my card. Call.

These stories were seldom firsthand, but usually from Bob by way of Ann who heard it over dinner with the P's. If you have ever been at a heated auction, then you have an idea of the boom fever. The auctioneer drives the price up, his every gesture saying: Act now! Act now! You folks are missing it! The room is tense with uncertainty, with desire. You're a fool not to bid; you're a fool to bid. You'll pay too much now; you'll pay far more in a month—if you even get the chance again. All the best land, all the best houses, jobs, stocks, places in private schools, they're going, going, gone. You shouda' been here last week, last year, five years ago, ten. Don't even, by chance, look at a decade-old newspaper. Houses were priced like today's new luxury cars. (After my brother had bought a new Volvo, my uncle said to my father, "Do you realize that your son has just spent more on a car than you did on your house?" "Yeah," my father answered, "but where can you go in a house?")

New Hampshire was an awfully poor state many times in its history: farms failed, textile mills failed, towns peaked in population before the Civil War and emptied out for a hundred years after. Pastures grew into forests; houses fell into cellars. In boom times New Hampshire acts like a poor-boy-made-good: He spends quickly on presents for ma, on cars and houses. And he talks constantly trying to convince himself that this time it's different.

We lived in New Hampshire during that mid-1980s boom. One percent unemployment, magazine stories touting the "miracle" and beating the drum for the state's fastest growing city as the-best-place-to-live-in-the-whole-damn-nation. We were renters, freelance writers. If the state was in an auction frenzy, we couldn't even get into the auction hall. Several times we went to look at houses with a real-estate agent. Decide right now or it's gone, they said. I don't even buy socks this fast. Or they said, that house you called about this morning: it's under agreement, it's sold. We sat down and sat it out.

During the boom we came to know a young couple who owned a deli. They lived that deli; their house adjoined the store. From the cash register to their bed was but a couple hundred steps.

The deli was an hour's drive from our house, on a state route that plunged south from the boom city, Nashua, to the Massachusetts border. Nashua was the fastest growing city in the second-fastest growing state east of the Mississippi River. The road had the feeling of an outpost: woods, then a store, then woods, then a small industrial garage, a strip mall of three stores, more woods, a lake, an old log cabin-like diner. Raw. On roads like this people are literally scratching for a living in sandpits, clear-cuts, swipes, and other chewings in the earth. There are small hot-dog stands in sandpits next to piles of logs. In other clearings, new houses, high on their foundations, sit naked in a bulldozer-made desert.

They talked with anticipation about how a big wave of development was headed their way from Nashua—it's what everyone said. This is the next growth corridor, they told us. They would sell their deli when the boom hit that road, and the scramble was on for the last bits of land. Their hard work would pay off. They had said this many times to themselves and others. The sentences were worn with use, a daily invocation.

We drove past there many months later. The deli was closed, and there was a for-sale sign. The boom city had gone bust, marooning the deli and the raw lots. The deli stood empty for years.

Our next-door neighbor lost his job, and then his house. It didn't happen quickly; it was a long free-fall. He was trying to sell his house for less than he had paid for it. There were no takers. No one was buying; the auction was over. On one stretch of road nearby almost every house was for sale. In another town, four of the five car dealers had closed. Our neighbor used up his pension. He learned how to dodge the bill collectors, how to string along the phone company and the electric company just enough to keep his lights and telephone. He was not blameless for his ruin, just unskilled for hard times. He had never looked for work in his entire career: head-hunters had lured him from company to company with ever higher six-figure salaries. He didn't know how to "make do"; he just made more money.

His car was the perfect symbol of New Hampshire's miracle economy. The three-year-old Jeep wagon, all trim, smart, and clean, was riding on tires so bald the wire cord was showing bright, and even passersby would say, Hey! Your tires—you'd better do something—that's dangerous. (An old friend eventually bought him tires.)

After the boom decade, New Hampshire led the nation in personal and business bankruptcies, and in the rise of people applying for food stamps. Banks were drowning in bad loans. Seventy-five percent of the state's banking assets were held in what were gingerly called "troubled banks." Economists said it was the worst recession for any region since the Great Depression. Many people were out of work and out of money in only ninety days. The national newspapers sought out those willing to publicly turn their empty pockets inside out. Their debt had helped finance the boom, their mortgage, car loans, and credit card debt. In the boom city the soup kitchen was besieged. "Middle-class people are coming in who would never have dreamed they would come to a soup kitchen," said the kitchen's director. "They still own a home but can't afford food."

That winter I remember driving past all the for-sale signs late at night. New Hampshire was crawling back into a deep sleep. Good night and slumber on in the houses of the men who made the Revolution and cleared the forests, the houses of men who went off to war down south, the houses of women who washed and canned and sewed through a thousand, thousand days of childbirth, fevered sleep, and blue-sky days of berry-picking. And now their houses stood empty along with the houses of the men and women who had made computer chips, who had consulted consultants who had advised other consultants on who to consult. In these houses they had sat and paid their Visa bills and car loans on the four-wheel-drive Jeeps, paid for the ski vacations, Caribbean holidays, and new additions with Cathedral ceilings, skylights, and Jacuzzis. They, too, had left their mark on New Hampshire.

And after a time it was our neighbor's turn. He declared bankruptcy; a bank in Texas owned his house. His house, built in the early years of the republic, and owned by one family for 125 years, now had a second address: it was "bundled" with other bad mortgages, the bank's specialty. This is a bad neighborhood for your home.

Neighbors had tried to help, offering to back a new mortgage, but it was too late. He was a prisoner of numbers: his house bought in boomtime had lost 40 percent of its value, while his variable mortgage rate kept climbing. The lines on the graph were headed the wrong way.

On a February morning, when it was all of five degrees, the bank's representatives arrived to auction off their house. Our neighbor was still living there, the tenant of a Texas bank. There were only a few people out in the bitter cold, and most of them were paid to be there: a real-estate agent who had been prowling our road for a half-hour sizing up everything (take your eyes off our house), the auctioneer who sold foreclosed houses all over the state (in bad times, his auction notices filled pages of the Sunday papers), and a fat lawyer who sat with the engine running in his black BMW for forty minutes. If you had seen this lawyer in a made-for-television movie, you'd say that he was a cliché, but there he was radiating arrogance.

In the icy road, the auctioneer set up a lectern with a microphone, and a table with information about the house, as he did when facing hundreds of people. It was odd, a lectern facing the frozen emptiness of the morning. One couple showed up to look at the house. The man said he'd picked up a "Victorian" on the cheap in another town, and he was looking to do that again. "All I want to know," he asked our neighbor, "is there anything wrong with it?" He asked another question about the venting under the eaves, a question that showed he didn't know anything about houses. Our neighbor made a sad face. He figured that this guy was a slumlord, he later told me.

The house was nearly empty inside. A moving van had arrived a week earlier. He had corralled what remained, his bed, desk, radio, and computer, in the living room. Next to his bed, he had placed a card he had printed on his computer. It stood up like a nameplate. "Things Change," it said. Under this, he had neatly printed in capital letters, DO NOT FEAR. And below this his name had been formally engraved, a gentleman's calling card.

After showing the house to the slumlord, our neighbor went outside and tried to say hello to the lawyer who was still sitting in his car. "Yeah, what do *you* want?" was all the lawyer said.

Our neighbor's real-estate agent showed up, and they talked about how they wished the house would have sold last summer and how they should have listed it with a much lower price. She asked after his dog, a handsome, if crazy, Airedale.

The auctioneer started the auction, noting that it was five degrees. I stood next to our neighbor and his real-estate agent. The other agent and the slumlord couple stood farther back. The lawyer had emerged from his car. There were no registered bidders. The lawyer came forward and bid the bottom price, buying it back for the bank. In three weeks the bank would let our neighbor know how long he could stay.

I went home and looked out my window about five minutes later. That corner of our road looked as it usually did, the old maples and pines as enigmatic as Mona Lisa's smile. No one was around. I felt as if the house had been witness to this one moment in its long history. Before our neighbor came along, the house had been in the same family since the Civil War.

We love old New England places. We look around and see an old house and tall pines and fields and trees beyond. But it is the landscape of numbers and finance that shadows old landscapes, creates new ones, and rules our days.

This is our heritage. These ghosts of boomtime New Hampshire join other ghosts, the farmers who lost it all in the "sheep mania" of the 1840s, the loggers and saw mills, the woolen and cotton mills, the railroad and canal investors, the back-to-the-landers who staked what little they had and their best years in a belief they could sustain themselves on soil that had defeated so many others. New Hampshire in its granite fastness shrugs off all schemes.

Walk a little ways and you'll find the failures in the woods, the cellar holes of once-proud homesteads, huge barns, well-built mills. Here's a partial list of cellar holes, monuments to toil and hope, from just one town history, Westminster, Massachusetts, 1893. Keep it handy. Post it the next time a boom comes your way and you hear from your neighbor what Bob heard from Ann about the great fortunes being made.

ABANDONED HOMESTEADS

A striking feature of the territory of the town at the present day ... is the appearance, here and there in all directions, of old cellars, wells, orchards or other tokens of dwellings once existing but now gone forever.

No. 1. In the extreme north part of the town, seemingly on 2nd Div., lot No. 112. Was purchased by Mark Cutter, in 1823, of Samuel Gibson of Pg., the house, barn, etc., then standing upon it. Mr. C. was in town 1815 and probably erected the buildings afterward occupied and finally owned by him. Subsequently to his death, about 1848, the family moved away. Several other parties resided there temporarily, afterwards, but the house disappeared many years since and nothing now remains, save the cellar and a few other tokens of what was once a well-appointed homestead.

No. 2. Situated half a mile north of the present residence of James H. Laws, on what was originally No. 41, 2d Div. It was the home of Isaac Brooks, who, coming from Acton in 1770, purchased land, erected a dwelling, etc., and spent his life there. After his death the buildings went to decay and at length disappeared, some years since.

No. 3. The residence of Samuel Brooks, son of Isaac, situated ab. 50 rods from the county road, on the town-way leading to his father's. A mill built by him is still standing.

No. 4. A small house once stood between the dwelling of Samuel Cooper (Now A. S. North's) and the old Martin (Chesmore) place. It was once occupied, by Wm. S. Bradbury, Benjamin Tilden, etc. Probably owned by Mr. Cooper.

No. 5. Located on lot 39, 2nd Div., in what is now an open field half a mile northwest of Mr. Laws. The dwelling was probably built by Jacob Harris, who bought the land of Samuel Kendall, O.P., in 1767, and who sold it, with house and improvements, to Jona. Brooks, Fg., 10 yrs. later. In 1779 Mr. Brooks sold to Jedh. Cooper. Only transients lived there afterwards and the buildings gradually went to decay.

No. 6. In 1772, Jacob Goodale, from Southboro', bought of David McIntyre, lot No. 5, 3d Div., and is supposed to have built a house upon it, which he occupied some 8 or 10 years and then left town. No corresponding cellar-hole or other token of a habitation has been found. . . .

No. 7. In the Nichols pasture, on the north side of the cross road leading from near where Porter F. Page lives to the valley, a few rods from the river, are there indications of the former residence of Thos. G. Cree, who was in town but a few years. His house was probably little more than a rude hut and soon disappeared.

No. 8. Half a mile east of the main highway over B. P. hill, at the end of a lane still traceable, are there the cellar, well, etc., which mark the site of the buildings of the large estate originally belonging to Jonathan Townsend, but sold by him to Nathl. Sawyer, from Reading, ab. 1773.

Mr. S. lived there till his decease and was succeeded by his son Eli, who sold to his son-in-law Joseph Burgess. The house was burned more than 50 years ago and the barn, in 1876.

No. 9. Some 50 rods in front of the Smyrna Whitney house on B. P. hill, are there evident signs of a former dwelling and accompanying farm buildings presumed to have been built by Darius Sawyer, who came to town from Lanc about 1770. . . .

No. 10. Half a mile eastwardly from the last mentioned locality are there similar tokens (unvisited) of an old family residence. One David Pratt bought lands of Dr. Zechariah Harvey ab. 1770 and, after erecting buildings, resided there till 1778, when he sold to S. Whitney, Jr. and left town.

The list continues to No. 101.

Asphalt, Mon Amour

An Alphabet of a Toxic Love Affair

Asphalt. (Asphalt Cement) "A dark brown to black cementitious material in which the predominating constituents are bitumens, which occur in nature or are obtained in petroleum processing. Asphalt is a constituent in varying proportions of most crude petroleum and used for paving, roofing, industrial and other special purposes."—Asphalt Institute.

It has been known as hot mix asphalt, blacktop, tarmac, macadam, plant mix, asphalt concrete, and bituminous concrete. Around 1900 various mixes were patented and sold under the trade names Bitulithic, Wilite, Romanite, National Pavement, Imperial, Indurite, and Macasphalt. Since the mid-1980s, "advanced paving materials" have been developed, including Open Graded Friction Course, Superpave, and Stone Matrix Asphalt (also known as Gap-Graded Superpave). From the Greek, *asphaltos:* secure, according to the Asphalt Education Partnership.

B.A. (Before Asphalt) In the first years of the new American republic, "each group of states lived a life apart," wrote Henry Adams. There was little interstate commerce. Mountains that are today a scenic Sunday drive were a barrier. Roads were rough: rutted and muddy in spring, impassable in winter, and an obstacle course of rocks and tree stumps in dry weather. Shipping a ton of goods thirty miles inland was as costly as shipping it to England. The mail between Boston and New York City took three days (using the better roads). A letter from Portland, Maine, to Louisville, Georgia, took twenty days. When Thomas Jefferson, on horseback, journeyed the one hundred miles from Monticello to Washington, he had to cross eight rivers, five of which had no bridges or boats.

"The union of New England with New York and Pennsylvania was not an easy task," wrote Adams, "but the union of New England with the Carolinas, and of the seacoast with the interior, promised to be a hopeless undertaking. . . . If Americans agreed in any opinion, they were united in wishing for roads."

Contraries. American place names run to contraries, said Walt Whitman. We name places for what we have destroyed (Farm View Estates). Asphalt is about creating contraries. No need to wonder why. We live by the bulldozer. We change everything around us. Each change leaves us further from the old order, from how-it-is. We hunger for the earth in its simplest alignment, the axis mundi of a great tree or rock, water running from a spring.

Depth. In 1960 the New Jersey Turnpike—"Tomorrow's Highway Today"—expanded its mileage with the deepest roadbed ever built in this country—three to four feet deep: a four-and-a-half inch "asphaltic concrete" top, a seven-and-a-half inch "macadam base," a six-and-a-half inch "gravel sub base," a five-and-a-half inch layer of "Grade A sand" on the inner lanes and ten inches on the outer lanes, and a final base of "Grade B sand."

Experiment. This is what we are adding to the land, water, and air: Alachlor, asphalt, atrazine, benzene, cadmium, carbon dioxide, chlorofluorocarbons, chromium, dioxin, formaldehyde, lead, mercury, nickel, nitrogen, PCBs, percholorethylene ("perc" for dry cleaning), plasticizers, radioactive waste, rubber, salt, sulfur oxide, vinyl chloride, zinc. This is an abbreviated list. We are adding these chemicals by the ton, in vast quantities that have only been with us since the end of World War II. Since 1940 chemical production worldwide has increased more than 350 times. (Pesticide use in the United States has doubled since Rachel Carson published *Silent Spring* in 1962.) These chemicals are little studied singly or in the many combinations in which we encounter them daily. There are between 45,000 and 100,000 chemicals in common use; no more than 3 percent have been tested to see if they are carcinogenic. (The government approves 80 percent of new chemicals in three weeks.) They are ubiquitous; accumulating, interfering with hormones, attacking immune systems, attaching to chromosomes. PCBs and other hormone-interrupting chemicals have been found in Arctic polar bears, weakening them and reducing their fertility. Women born between 1947 and 1957 have nearly a three-times greater risk for breast cancer than their great-grandmothers did. One in four hundred Americans can expect to develop cancer before age fifteen. One in two American men will develop cancer in his life. For women, the probability of developing cancer is one in three. These chemicals are in our soil and water, in our lungs, in our blood and bones. (The average American body is likely to have at least five hundred synthetic chemicals.) We are living in a great experiment.

"One errant Old World primate species is now changing the global environment more than that environment has changed at any previous time since the end of the Mesozoic Era sixty-five million years ago," says the eminent biologist E. O. Wilson.

Free. Land, water, air: What was once free is now for sale. And what's polluted can also be sold. Here's an example: If you own an electric power plant you can sell pollution. It is not phrased that way. If you have not polluted to the limit set by law, you can sell the so-called "unused emissions" to another power plant far away. They can buy the "credits" and keep polluting, rather than cleaning up the air. The emission permits for sulfur dioxide—a key cause of acid rain—are traded as a commodity on the Chicago Board of Trade. (Some in the industry call them "excess cleanliness credits.") One pollution trader believes that carbon dioxide has a great future. "Given the level of global emissions, this could become the largest commodity market in the world."

Too bad for you if you live by the polluting plant. There's no free market for your lungs. Every breath you take underwrites my profit. Your health has been sold out to subsidize my factory.

God. "O Almighty God, who has given us this earth and has appointed men to have domination over it; who has commanded us to make straight the highways, to lift up the valleys and to make the mountains low, we ask thy blessing upon these men who do just that. Fill them with a sense of accomplishment, not just for the roads built, but for the ways opened for the lengthening of visions, the broader hopes and the greater joys which makes these highways a possibility for mankind.

"Bless these, our Nation's road builders, and their friends. For the benefits we reap from their labors, we praise thee; may thy glory be revealed in us. Amen."—"Prayer for America's Road Builders," the official prayer of the American Road Builders' Association, 1965.

Happiness. Is there an index of happiness that recedes as we add more chemicals to the world? Does happiness exist in an inverse ratio to paving?

The first good roads were a relief. They brought ease of travel to the countryside. Farmers could more easily ship their produce, meet with neighbors, get to town on market day. But the next mile, and the one after that, eat us alive. The "pursuit of happiness"—whatever Mr. Jefferson meant by that phrase—is a tar pit.

Ideal. In the beginning there was the joy of travel—for the wealthy. Here is Edith Wharton in 1908, writing of her "motor-flight through France": "The motor-car has restored the romance of travel. Freeing us from all the compulsions and contacts of the railway, the bondage to fixed hours and the beaten track, the approach to each town through the area of ugliness and desolation created by the railway itself, it has given us back the wonder, the adventure and the novelty which enlivened the way of our posting grandparents. Above all these recovered pleasures must be ranked the delight of taking a town unawares, stealing on it by back ways and unchronicled paths, and surprising in it some intimate aspect of past time, some silhouette hidden for half a century or more by the ugly mask of railway embankments and the iron bulk of a huge station. Then the villages that we missed and yearned for from the windows of the train—the unseen villages have been given back to us!"

This is the dream world of automobile advertising: you're alone on the open road, the two-lane blacktop through amber waves of grain, or curling tight on a rise overlooking the Pacific, or freed from all roads, ripping across the desert, climbing steep mesas and smashing through streams.

Jaywalking. "The pedestrian was a most serious hindrance," said one traffic engineer in the 1920s.

Kicks. "Get your kicks . . . on Route 66!" Jack Kerouac, author of *On The Road,* never had a driver's license. Robert Moses, builder of more than thirty highways and seven major bridges, also never had a driver's license. Woodrow Wilson would have preferred that no one had a driver's license. In 1906 Wilson, then a college president, wanted to ban cars. "To the country-man they are a picture of the arrogance of wealth, with all its independence and carelessness. . . . Nothing has spread social-istic feeling more than the use of the automobile," said Wilson. As a Southerner, he said, he could understand those who shot hit-and-run drivers.

Land. Highways turn land into time. Here's one small example. For five miles of new road bypassing a village, New Hampshire's highway engineers moved two million tons of earth and applied 72,000 tons of asphalt. The engineers spent $33 million. They are creating more than roads; they are creating new landscapes. They have heaped up steep hillsides of crushed stone and mounded earthen bunkers as if they intended to defend the bypass from tank attack. Where else do we commit millions of dollars to shape the land? The village has been freed from traffic, and drivers now save about ten minutes or so on their commute to the state capital. That's the equation: land churned into time. Place erosion. Hills leveled, bogs filled, for access. Here is bulldozed to look like there.

To build the first 427 miles of the New York State Thruway, enough earth was moved to make a wall around the equator six feet wide and two-and-a-half feet high. To build the Interstate highway system, enough earth was moved "to bury all of Connecticut two feet deep," said President Dwight Eisenhower.

Magic. The cover of the April 1966 issue of Asphalt—"a quarterly publication of the Asphalt Institute"—shows "Asphalt's Magic Circle." Four arrows form a circle:

1. Deep-strength asphalt pavement provides more paved roads for fewer tax dollars.
2. More paved roads stimulate travel, boost road fuel use, provide more road-tax revenue.
3. More road-tax revenue means more dollars to maintain and build extra paved roads.
4. More improved roads ease traffic congestion and develop even more travel.

Back to number one and refrain endlessly.

"In short, we have a self-perpetuating cycle, the key element of which is new paved roads," said *Asphalt* in 1967. "The 45,000 new miles added to the road and street network each year accommodate automotive travel, generate fuel consumption, produce road-building revenue. Scratch the new roads and the cycle ceases to function. Three million new vehicles surging into the traffic stream each year without new paved mileage to provide necessary running room: the spectacle is too miserable to contemplate."

Nature. Drive, don't hike. "If our generation and succeeding ones become—as seems likely—more and more conscious of beauty, it will be because every road that is built can and should make beauty accessible to more people. In a year's time, a few hundred people may be able to afford the time and the energy to *hike* through a woods or a park. But every day, hundreds of *thousands* may *drive* through those woods and parks, when carefully designed highways unfurl the whole, lovely view," said H. E. Humphreys Jr., an executive of the U. S. Rubber Company. He was addressing the Eleventh Highway Transportation Congress in 1967 about the "anguished cries from some about paving the countryside."

Odometer. Since 1970 the population of the United States has increased 32 percent; "vehicle miles traveled" have increased four times faster, rising 131 percent. The average American drives 14,000 miles a year. "I move, therefore I am" is the American notion of existence, says Jane Holtz Kay in *Asphalt Nation.*

Paving. A short history. The first asphalt was found in lakes, or mixed with sand and limestone. The Phoenicians caulked their ships with asphalt and "the infant Moses' basket was waterproofed with asphalt," says the Asphalt Education Partnership. (The translations most of us read called it "pitch.") Ancient Babylonians are recorded as paving the first road with asphalt around 625 B.C.

In America, some streets were paved with coal tar in the 1860s and 1870s, others with cobblestones, granite blocks, or wooden blocks soaked in creosote (which are believed to have spread the great Chicago fire of 1871). Most streets were a sorry mess. "The street is not passable, nor is it jackassable," said a sign posted in Santa Ana, California. "All who travel it must turn out and gravel it."

A Belgian chemist laid down the country's first asphalt pavement in Newark, New Jersey, in 1870. He then went on to Washington to pave Pennsylvania Avenue in 1876 with asphalt imported from Trinidad (which has the world's largest natural asphalt lake). Other cities took note. New York, Buffalo, Philadelphia, and San Francisco experimented with the new pavement. Indianapolis hosted the first-ever "Paving Exposition" in 1890, attracting 500 officials from other cities. Asphalt was the new standard. "In some cities—as in Baltimore, for example—paving with cobblestones is prohibited by law, like murder, theft, and drunkenness," reported one urban reformer in 1901.

The new roads saved money. In 1910 the Annals of the American Academy calculated the cost of hauling one ton with horse and wagon over one level mile:

On asphalt the cost of hauling is: $2.70
On stone paving, dry and in order: $5.33
On stone paving covered with mud: $21.30
On broken-stone, with ruts and mud: $26.00
On earth, dry and hard: $18.00
On earth, with ruts and mud: $39.00
On gravel loose: $51.60
On sand, dry: $64.00

Most road building had been local, the business of towns. In the years before World War I, as the price of the Model T fell, new national associations called for better roads. Congress refused to fund a system of national roads in 1912, calling it a frivolous expense "for the benefit of a few wealthy pleasure seekers." In 1913 the Lincoln Highway Association, a private group, began raising money to build the nation's first transcontinental highway. Only 7 percent of the nation's roads were paved. Oil companies started producing artificial asphalt, and by 1907 the refined product was used more than asphalt mined in natural deposits.

Cars were overwhelming cities—motor vehicle registration had jumped 1,000 percent. In 1910 Detroit surrendered Cadillac Square for a parking lot. New York cut in half the park in

Park Avenue in 1921, shaving the central mall. In 1924 Andrew Mellon, the secretary of the Treasury, proposed moving the Washington Monument to make room to park cars. Science fiction stories, movies, and architects' plans featured cities with multiple tiers of traffic racing through skyscrapers. Robert Moses proposed a Mid-Manhattan Expressway in 1950, which would have gone right through the Empire State Building at the sixth or seventh floor.

Progressive reformers looked to the motorcar to break the trolley company monopolies, relieve crowded cities, and free the streets from the mire and stink of tons of horse manure. (In 1880, Kansas City removed street muck only when it was more than three inches deep.) Tentatively, the federal government began to fund road construction in 1916 and 1921. After World War II, the government took the lead. The Federal-Aid Highway Act of 1956 committed America to building 41,000 miles of new highways. The new roads followed "desire lines"—the desire by drivers for the shortest routes. Neighborhoods, parks, and waterfront were lost to the largest peacetime public works project in the world's history. "When you operate in an overbuilt metropolis you have to hack your way with a meat ax," Robert Moses told the National Highway Users Conference in 1964.

Asphalt production boomed, setting new records as the Interstate grew. "The total pavement of the system would make a parking lot big enough to hold two thirds of all the automobiles in the United States," President Eisenhower said. "The amount of concrete poured to form these roadways would build eighty Hoover Dams or six sidewalks to the moon. . . . More than any single action by the government since the end of the war, this would change the face of America."

Today there are 38.4 million acres of roads and parking lots in the United States, a paved area nearly the size of two Irelands.

Quantity. We need to redefine plenty, to reintroduce the word "enough." *("I have enough things.")* The cornucopia, the old horn of plenty that survives in classroom Thanksgiving decorations, has come to represent a harvest of products—more computers, larger cars and televisions and houses. The real harvest is clean water and fresh air. Things displace time, and time is all that we are given, all that we have. Clean water, fresh air, the earth itself, and our numbered days to sing its praises: plenty.

Recipe. "Ever wondered what asphalt tastes like? If you make it right, it tastes like chocolate and peanut butter!" says the Asphalt Education Partnership in its suggested lesson plans for teachers. "This recipe [Hot Mix Asphalt Candy] is a great way to show kids how asphalt is made. The oatmeal and peanuts are the aggregate and the chocolate/peanut butter mixture is the asphalt binder." The Asphalt Education Partnership offers other recipes for the home kitchen, including "Hot Mix Snackers," "Kickin' Asphalt and Takin' Names Chili," and "Open Road Cake"—"To decorate your next cake with an authentic asphalt feel, regular chocolate frosting just won't do. Here's how you can pave a cake with the real look of asphalt."

Sacred. Springs, trees, and rocks were once believed to be holy. "There is in fact no spring that is not sacred," wrote the Roman Servius. Springs were powerful places of healing. An 1895 survey of Ireland counted three thousand springs. Sacred groves stood in many places and were often used for worship. In Celtic, *Doire* is an oakwood, a word we know as Derry. In 1851 Ireland had one thousand "townlands" named Derry. Some rocks were holy. In the 1600s Lithuanians kept stones at home as sacred altars. They were among the last holdouts of the old religion. The new religion chased out the old spirits, leveled the old groves. St. Boniface cut down the great Oak of Jupiter around 723; the Society of Jesus destroyed Lithuania's sacred oaks in the 1500s. The new religion was an urban religion; it despised the worship of a tree or a rock or a spring. It did not worship a place.

"Once upon a time, when people were decent, everyone had *un qrana fé* [a great faith] in these stones: everyone prayed to them and worshipped them," a peasant in a remote valley of the Pyrenees told an anthropologist and a Curé (a parish priest) in 1877. "Following a remark by the Curé the old man cried out in a voice vibrating with emotion, 'You may not believe in these stones, Monsieur le Curé, but *I* do. I believe in them as all my ancestors did and two of today's men are not the equal of the men of those days.'"

Toxic. A reckoning of the pollution created by one small (Ford Escort-sized) car, according to a study by the Environment and Forecasting Institute in Heidelberg:

1. Building the car accounts for one-third of the environmental cost. Before it has even driven one mile, one car makes 29 tons of waste and 1,207 million cubic yards of polluted air.
2. Driving the car is another 60 percent of the environmental cost. Traveling 85,000 miles produces 1,330 million cubic yards of polluted air and 40 pounds of shed rubber, brake linings, and broken road surface.
3. Junking it is 7 percent: 133 million cubic yards of polluted air, plus PCBs and hydrocarbons.

Global warming scorecard: 66 tons of carbon dioxide (15 tons in manufacturing, 45 tons from driving, and 6 tons from junking it). Cars cause one half of global warming. (Concentrations of atmospheric carbon dioxide are 50 percent higher than before the Industrial Revolution.)

By 2020, the number of cars in the world is expected to double to one billion.

"To rephrase an environmental slogan, if you got caught driving a car across state lines, you'd go to jail for transporting toxic waste," writes Jane Holtz Kay in *Asphalt Nation*.

Utopia. "Metropolis. Utopia. EXIT 2 MILES"—test sign for the new Interstate highway system, circa 1957. It would take more than one exit to accommodate the many automobile Utopias. Edgar Chambless proposed Roadtown in 1910. Take the skyscraper and lay it down across the countryside, said Chambless.

The road is on the roof, apartments in the middle, trains run through the continuous basement—and everyone has a back-yard. In the 1920s and 1930s Le Corbusier promoted similar road/buildings for Rio and Algiers as "vertical garden cities." G. A. Jellicoe published *Motopia* in 1961—a countryside cut into a Cartesian grid of road-buildings. (Cars on the roof again.) But it was General Motors that triumphed with Futurama at the New York World's Fair in 1939: skyscrapers lining highways with more than a dozen lanes of teardrop-shaped cars speeding along at 100 miles an hour. "Strange? Fantastic? Unbelievable?" asked the Futurama narrator. "Remember, this is the world of 1960."

Victim. Blaming the victim is the way we deal with the huge increase in cancer, says biologist Sandra Steingraber, who has had bladder cancer. She compares the brochures often found in doctors' waiting rooms with medical textbooks. The brochures put the burden on the individual; the textbooks do not. Brochure: "Today it is known that about 80 percent of cancer cases are tied to the way people live their lives," says the U.S. Department of Health and Human Services. Textbook: "As much as 90 percent of all forms of cancer is attributable to specific environmental factors," says *Human Genetics: A Modern Synthesis.* Brochure: "You can control many of the factors that cause cancer. . . . You can decide how you're going to live your life— which habits you will keep and which ones you will change." Textbook: "Reducing or eliminating exposures to environmental carcinogens would dramatically reduce the prevalence of cancer in the United States." These brochures presume "that the ongoing contamination of our air, food, and water is an immutable fact of the human condition to which we must accommodate ourselves," writes Steingraber. "When we are urged to 'avoid carcinogens in the environment and work-place,' this advice begs the question: Why are there known carcinogens in our environment and at our job sites in the first place?"

In her home state, heavily industrial Illinois, "no attempt is made to correlate cancer statistics with the Toxic Release Inventory data (the amounts reported to the government of some 654 toxic chemicals released into the environment by certain manufacturers)." And thus, we keep the two separate; our toxic love affair with all these products, and illness.

World. "Thinkest thou Pierre that the whole world will one day be paved?"

"Oh no that can never be." — Herman Melville, *Pierre, or the Ambiguities* (1852).

Between 500 and 550 million tons of asphalt are used annually in America.

X, Y, and Z. The as-yet unnamed cities and towns we will build. "The world population is going to double. We have to build this world all over again," says architect David Howard. He's an advocate for building new, compact villages using the principles of the New England village. "The whole nineteenth century and early twentieth century was a process of building villages. We're just not building villages anymore." Do not dismiss these places because they do not yet exist. In X people will be born to prosper or struggle. In Y people will dream and write poems about Y's beauty and sorrows. Children from Z will grow up and go to war to defend their country, to defend the world they love in Z. We should build these new towns with great care, and less asphalt.

Welcome to the | Blueblood Milltown

"Quintessential"

Peterborough, New Hampshire, is a good town to live in. That's what the signs say at the town line. This is not so much a boast or a wish as it is the credo of the men and women who remade Peterborough in the era of World War I. This is the calling card of an elite group of reformers. The signs were a dedication and a promise: This will be a good town once we change it. In a sense, these signs are another historic marker: The Progressive Era lived here, they could say. Or: Welcome to the Blueblood Milltown.

At the close of the nineteenth century, Peterborough was just another milltown, one of the little Lowells that grew from the power of the Contoocook River. The mills in Peterborough made cloth, woodenware, and baskets. And like almost all of New England's mills, they were losing out to newer mills with cheaper labor down south.

Peterborough, like many New Hampshire towns, was first settled on a hill with glorious views but moved downhill to the river and power. Milltowns are shaped by the power of water falling. The height of the falls determines the size of the head-races, waterwheels, and tailraces. The mills build as close to a river as needed. All the rest—housing for workers and over-seers, a church or two, a store or two, and the streets—what we would call a village—is usually an afterthought. The mill is planned; the rest just happens. Like other small mill villages, Peterborough had the hard look of new places, as if the land had been snapped like a blanket, so that brick churches, gran-ite storerooms, and wooden framed houses were all a little askew, bumping up against each other along the dirt streets.

The first mill in 1793 set up by the falls of the Nubanusit River, and the rest of the village crowded in around it. The tail-race from that mill, where the water ran to return to the Con-toocook River, was known as the Little Jordan. The Baptist church backed up on the tailrace and used the water for bap-tisms in a show of pragmatic holiness. The mills are long gone, but the town is still honeycombed with buried tailraces and canals. This buried history reasserts itself any time the ground is opened, or, quite dangerously, when a gasoline spill in the winter of 2003 quickly spread into the Little Jordan, closing the town.

That early mill burned down, and in 1829 the Phoenix fac-tory was rebuilt as an up-to-date, four-story brick mill with two handsome bell towers framing the entrance. In the last quarter of the nineteenth century, the Phoenix Mill made textiles, but ran only intermittently. It had become what they called a "high cost mill." The mill closed in 1908, and various businesses tried to make a go of it, making excelsior, chairs, and clothespins. For several years a steam laundry occupied part of the mill. By 1916 the large, empty mill dominated Peterborough's central village. A new group of owners bought the Phoenix Mill that year, incorporated as the Old Phoenix Mill Associates, and they were unlike the other owners. They were summer people, Harvard professors, wealthy heiresses, people with money made in Boston and Chicago, and they wanted to produce a different product than cloth or chairs; they wanted to produce a new town.

Four streets at the meeting of two rivers: Main, Grove, School, and Depot Streets. This was the town's center. School and Depot, by the railroad and the Old Shoe Factory, were the back streets. Main and Grove were the home to churches, banks, stores, a tavern, the post office, and the town hall known as the opera house. The empty Phoenix Mill stood over it all, meeting Main Street close behind the town hall, and facing Grove Street with its bell towers and millyard.

For the wealthy new owners, the empty mill was a symptom of what they were fighting. New England was in decline. This was common knowledge. The magazines they read and wrote for had been reporting the bad news for years. The *North American Review,* the *Nation, New England Magazine, Putnam's Monthly,* and others wrote about "The Decay of New England Thought" (1881), "The Decay of New England Churches" (1887), and "The Rural Degeneracy Cry" (1907). They asked, "What's the Matter with New England?"(1907) and "What Ails New England?" (1909). New England was "the National Wallflower" (1916). New Hampshire, with its abandoned farms, was "a state for sale at $10 an acre" (1905).

One leading businessman confided privately, "It is no use, New England has seen her best days. It is only a question of time before our industries will disappear as fast as the farms are going at present. Our future lies with the tourist and the summer boarder. As a productive section of the country, New England is doomed. Of course, in public I boost New England, but for all that, I realize that the situation is hopeless."

The Old Phoenix Mill Associates saw a different future. They had a vision of rural uplift, which called for village improvement, living up to colonial ideals, managing farms on a scientific or business plan, and cultivating the arts to promote tourism, says geographer Scott Roper in his careful study of the Associates.

"If our industries decline and our farms continue to be abandoned, if we become nothing more than a summer playground, it will not be because our problem is unsolvable or our situation inherently hopeless, but because the old spirit of resourcefulness and determination has died out," said Associate Robert P. Bass. He was answering the gloomy, unnamed businessman whom he had quoted. "We must direct all effort to best advantage, we must pull together. Our water powers must be developed, those industries best adapted to our resources and markets must be encouraged, our lands and forests must be more efficiently cultivated and husbanded, our people must be educated and organized to a new efficiency and a new spirit of cooperation. It means a higher type of civilization, it requires more resourcefulness, more unselfishness."

Bass and the other Associates were committed to creating this "higher type of civilization." Bass had served one term as New Hampshire's governor. A political novice, the thirty-six-year-old had run on a reform platform against an old corrupt political machine that was run by the Boston & Maine Railroad. The Boston & Maine was a monopoly, the only railroad in New England. In New Hampshire, the railroad chose the candidates for governor and reviewed and approved all legislation. The railroad had almost every lawyer in the state under retainer and almost every newspaper under control. It ruled by handing out free railroad passes. Each state representative rode for free. "New Hampshire," said the Progressive lawyer Louis Brandeis, "has been a state within the Boston & Maine." For thirty years there had been attempts to free the state from railroad rule. In 1910 Bass, backed by a small group of reformers, the Lincoln Republicans, won a surprising victory. In an astonishing season of reform that stands as one of the great achievements of the Progressive Era, the young governor fulfilled his promises to the voters. He created one of the first Public Service Commissions in the country to regulate the railroad and other utilities, and he enacted effective laws for child labor, factory inspection, pure food, and workmen's compensation. He expanded forest reserves and reformed campaign finance.

All contributions had to be made public, and corporate contributions were prohibited.

Bass had summered in Peterborough as a boy before moving there after graduating from Harvard. Independently wealthy, he managed the family's Chicago real estate from his Peterborough farm. His mother, Clara F. Bass, had grown up in Chicago but brought her family back to their ancestral home each summer. Her ancestors had been leaders among the town's early settlers, and she took a keen interest in Peterborough. She was one of the founders of the historical society and donated a new building, which was pivotal in changing the town.

The Basses hired another Associate to design the historical society building, Boston architect Benjamin Franklin W. Russell. He had bought the town's old poor farm for a summer home. The Associates kept big farms, summer estates they displayed on tours. They wanted to show the local farmers that modern practices could make farms profitable. Russell was proud that he had increased his hay production from four or five tons to seventy-five tons in ten years. His Guernsey cows supplied milk for the local schools. Russell figured that the Associates as a group paid nearly 25 percent of Peterborough's property tax.

Russell had fallen for the town. "I have practiced my profession for twenty years in a great many communities and I like to make money; but in Peterborough I like to practice it just for its own sake, even though I actually lose money," Russell wrote in a letter. "I often wonder why and have made up my mind that it is because the town and its people are so fine and so unusual that there is a satisfaction greater than money there."

The Basses and Russell were the most active of the eighteen founding stockholders of the Old Phoenix Mill Associates. They were representative of an elite that acted for the town but without seeking public comment or approval. They remade the town with a minimum of public explanation. They did not write letters to the editor, display their plans, or, as we say today, "welcome input." They came forward to speak at the dedication of a cornerstone or a new building, or when the use of public money required them to appear before a town meeting.

Peterborough was a place they chose for summer living, just as they chose other places in different seasons. The Associates planned Peterborough's future in letters that flew from Boston to Bermuda, to a New York hotel and a North Carolina resort. They regarded Peterborough as their own discovery, a frontier outpost on the map of fashionable addresses, a new world to shape.

Many businesses wanted to buy or lease the Phoenix Mill. A Massachusetts mill offered to buy the building, land, and water rights to produce worsted yarn. "We would take as much pride in the appearance of the property as you or your associates could well desire," said the company.

Any other landlord of a vacant mill would have welcomed this offer. The Associates did not. "While it seems too bad to have a good water power and a manufacturing plant in the middle of Peterborough idle . . . I do not see how [this] offer, reasonable as it is, could be accepted," associate Fred Rice wrote from Boston. "Since so much recently has been invested in buildings to make the center of Peterborough attractive, I believe it would be a step backward to allow this property to be used for mill purposes again." Using the old mill for manufacturing would be inconsistent with the original idea that had brought the Associates together, he said.

The Associates' treasurer, a Boston manufacturer, agreed. The mill was too far from a railroad siding to be profitable, he said. "And while I believe firmly in industries for our town, it should be encouraged at some point more distant from the center of the village, and convenient to transportation."

The yarn manufacturer, learning of their objections, withdrew his offer but told them that if they changed their mind, he was interested. He preferred Peterborough to any other place he was considering, he said.

There were other inquiries from a match company, a Peterborough textile mill, the local newspaper, a garage, and the American Guernsey Cattle Club, the registry for the breed, which was looking to expand its offices in town. They refused all offers, keeping to their plans for improving Peterborough. They tore down the mill's later additions to clean up the mill-yard and deeded some of the land to new buildings on Grove Street. They also planned to tear down the old brick-end mill housing, which one associate, in a national publication, had called "a most objectionable group of tenements."

Some of that land was given to the Basses for the new historical society building on Grove Street. Russell, the architect, worked with the Basses, convincing them that a red-brick Colonial Revival, or Georgian, building fit "the spirit of the town." A few months after the plans were ready, there was a fire in the opera house, which was next door to the planned historical society. Russell hired an engineer who produced a report showing that the damage from this and two earlier fires was so extensive "that it would be very stupid for the Town to try to repair it." This report convinced a special town meeting to build a new Town House. Russell and Robert Bass were appointed to the building committee. Russell, with his architectural partner J. Lovell Little, designed a new Town House modeled on Boston's Faneuil Hall, the "storied cradle of New England liberty and democracy." The committee (with Russell abstaining) voted for the design.

The look of the new Peterborough, "the good town to live in," was set. The same contractor and same "hard-burned, dark-red, water-struck bricks" would be used in both buildings. The new look would be unified, orderly, and dressed in the colonial past. Other buildings followed quickly. Across the street from the historical society, Little and Russell designed a close colonial cousin for the American Guernsey Cattle Club. A few years later the Peterborough Savings Bank next door, which was housed in a post–Civil War Second Empire building, remodeled its first-floor facade in the accepted colonial fashion. Other architects maintained the dress code with a red brick First National Bank and a Post Office.

This is the formal street that the Old Phoenix Mill Associates built. For them, the colonial past was the real New England. The industrial New England that had thrived on the profits of the Civil War was a wrong turn, and its dying mills were sapping the region, leaving it with ugly tenements housing immigrants.

New England could be revived if it returned to the principles of the founding fathers. The new Town House could show the way, said Russell at the Town House's dedication in 1918. "The Town House has been conceived and wrought in the spirit of our ancestors,—simple, dignified, unpretentious. Let it teach us such qualities, that we shall hand down an heritage to our children . . . Let us make its surroundings attractive and have a centre in Peterborough such as those of the finest old New England towns! Let us not only do this but also have the Town House stand as an example and inspiration for each home, each structure in town. Then, every unsightly, poorly-kept building which is now on our streets . . . will be changed or will disappear. . . . Peterborough will then be worthy of her early settlers, and those who have struggled to make it what it is, and worthy of those who live here now.

"We could not have constructed a public building in a more inspiring time. The world is moving to a higher level. If we do not move with it we shall be left far behind and lose our great opportunities. Soon, peace is coming for this troubled world," Russell said, and with the end of the Great War would come new responsibilities. "Our boys have cheerfully given up home, friends, everything, aye,—some of them their lives, for what this Town House stands for. Let us do our share and show that we understand and appreciate what they have done and that it is all worthwhile, by making our town and our every action finer and better than ever before. We must do this, for our generation and those who follow it are going to be measured by new standards. The heroism of Belgium, the glory of France, the valor of England, the gallantry of Italy, the unselfishness of America, are showing the world that ideals are the truest and greatest forces on earth."

For these New Hampshire reformers, eighteenth-century architecture was progressive. The bumptious milltown Second Empire buildings, the style that took hold during the Civil War, was rude. The Second Empire is a striver's architecture—the buildings hunched and narrow, reaching, exaggerating height with tall windows and doors, and towers topped with metal work. It's a style that can overreach even in the smallest house on a tiny lot. When the Second Empire fell from fashion, it was as stale as old cigar smoke, the exhaled pretensions of another era. Edward Hopper's paintings caught the spookiness of these fallen empires.

Peterborough's antipathy to the Second Empire lasts to this day, as the town leveled an imposing mansion in the 1970s and a former Main Street pharmacy in the 1980s. (A Gothic Revival cottage was rescued in the 1990s after an acrimonious debate.) The town continued to build offices and banks in a wan Colonial Revival, an off-the-rack Colonial Williamsburg. The style has stuck.

The Associates praised their own work in a 1926 booklet showing the new buildings, as well as their own estates. "Peterborough people are justly proud of the strikingly unique group of central buildings—a colony that draws the attention of the casual visitor no less than it has drawn the admiration of architects and town planners from a distance. Of ivy-grown weathered red brick, gray granite, and white woodwork, they are at once impressive and appropriate to the village. . . . The entire group, though of recent construction, adds greatly to the charm of a town that is already typical of the colonial beauty of central New England."

This is the Peterborough people see today. Visitors who don't know the words "Colonial Revival" like the red brick buildings. They are familiar, dignified, old—but not that old. This is what their bank or ice-cream parlor back home may look like. This is what they believe a New England village should look like. It is a stage set for their expectations.

Peterborough is "the quintessential New England village, with handsome red-brick public buildings and the type of

natural settings you see depicted in Currier and Ives prints,"
reported the authors of *Safe Places for the 80s*. ("Don't tell a
soul—just move there, now!" implored the book's cover.) So
many other examples can be quoted that it's as if the English
language had shriveled to a handful of words like quaint and
charming.

Other towns have made the leap from mill work to the life-
after. Many other New England towns are still struggling, trying to find a use for the empty mills, trying to create a new
image. Peterborough made the leap earlier than most towns
and made the leap with old manners. This is what some hold
against Peterborough—it has jumped class, put on airs, dressed
up for Sunday dinner and burnt the overalls.

"Industrially, the town is going forward but not to such an
extent that 'Our Town' is, or likely ever will be, 'just another
mill town,'" said a 1950 brochure.

Is there a hauteur in Peterborough's manner? The town *has*
a manner. How many other towns do?

Hobbyville

Many villages "are now inhabited by a conservative folk, limited in experience, homely in their ways, wedded to old customs, reluctant to change anything, indifferent to progress,
niggardly with their money for sanitary and aesthetic purposes; and many such villages are extravagant with franchises
to all sorts of companies, to which they give permission to hack
trees, to tear up roads, and to disfigure streets with unsightly
poles and wires, regardless of the added expense they bring
upon the town," Mary Caroline Bobbins wrote in the *Atlantic*
in 1897. "That some effort is necessary to stir the townsfolk
from their time-worn content is evident, and we have cause for
rejoicing that in many of our rural New England communities
the awakening has come through the presence of summer visitors and residents, who bring with them from the city habits of
comfort and convenience which are shocked by old-time country makeshifts. . . . Village improvement is thus the offspring of

the cities, and in most cases it is paid for and engineered by those who have enjoyed city advantages." Summer people, the city mice of the old Beatrix Potter story, have largely created what we think of as the country.

"The summer pilgrim seeking a retired rural retreat, and the victim of the slack-baked bread, the white doughy pie, the close room, the feather-bed, the general discomfort and taste-lessness which have characterized so much country life, hail with delight the advent of the Village Improvement Societies and the Sanitary Associations of recent years," wrote the editor of *Harper's New Monthly Magazine* in 1882.

Village improvement societies began in a few New England towns before the Civil War, and by the last decades of the nine-teenth century they were a topic of national discussion. Village improvement is a mix of sanitation and aesthetics. It's all on the agenda, from horseflies to civic art: plant trees, plan parks, pave streets; start evening lecture series, libraries, little art museums; build colonial-style town halls and post offices in a group to have the best effect; cover manure piles with lime. Clean up the mess made by the railroad, the mill, and the horse. Banish the annoyance of muck and mud, the flies everywhere spreading disease.

The improvement societies had their feet in the muck and their eyes on the big city and Europe. "We mean to work till every street shall be graded, every sidewalk shaded, every noxious weed eradicated, every water-course laid and per-fected, and every nook and corner beautified—in short till art combined with nature shall have rendered our town the most beautiful and attractive of our ancient commonwealth," said the founders of the nation's second village improvement society in Stockbridge, Massachusetts, in 1853.

"Rural uplift" is what they sometimes called it, an earnest project to advance "the progress of the race." "There is nothing more contagious than a good example," wrote Parris Thaxter Farwell in *Village Improvement* (1913). A clean barn leads to clean morals. Scrub a child, send him home, and the mother will clean up her kitchen. Show a man good prints of the best

European masters and he may forsake the saloon. "It is a splendid thing for a community year after year, generation after generation, to be trained in the love of decency, beauty, and good taste. . . . The 'hoodlum,' the 'tough,' does not thrive in towns where boys are reared in the love of natural beauty and trained to recognize and cultivate it."

Snobbery and democracy are all mixed up in this faith: let everyone join in—it's good for them. "Some of the older villages in the Eastern States are pathetic spectacles of struggle between a disappearing native population and an invasion of foreign families not yet trained in neatness and thrift," wrote Farwell. "If there happens to be a foreign section, of Italians, for example, or of Poles, they should be officially represented on the society's executive committee." It's a kind of camouflaged elitism—rural uplift ratified by the masses. "In time" they "will learn how to find pleasure in the things that are beautiful." Village improvement is also village simplification. In attempting to clean up the mess of commerce do we also root out vitality? What did Peterborough lose when the "objectionable" tenements were torn down?

Improvement is an American preoccupation: the Sunday sermon, Benjamin Franklin's Poor Richard, Ralph Waldo Emerson's essays. Abolition, Prohibition, wars on poverty and cancer and drugs, diets, crusades, Utopias, protests, calls to action, days of prayer, teach-ins, moratoriums, boycotts, petitions, letter-writing campaigns, Hands-Across-America, concerts in aid of causes, celebrities sprouting consciences before our eyes telling us about diseases we could cure if we would commit enough money. . . . America is a continental-sized improvement project. Self-improvement, betterment, home improvement, village improvement—this is the wheel we turn from crisis to reform to crisis. This is civic life on the American plan, an urgent do-it-yourself project to build a life raft.

Behind all village improvement sleeps Rip Van Winkle. He rises after twenty years of sleep in the hills and comes home to a town he can't recognize. No one knows him. He is a stranger in his native realm, an exile on Main Street. The village reformers

of the late nineteenth and early twentieth centuries were trying to get their towns to behave, their railroad-addled landscapes to settle, just for a moment or two, in the commercial
upheaval. They wanted their towns to stop changing and
changing again until they were strangers at home.

Peterborough was the hobby of rich summer people. In the
Village Improvement Era, the 1890s to the 1920s, the Associates gave the town a hospital, playground, public golf course
and clubhouse, nursery school, a church by a national architect, a war memorial (backed by public subscription), a rebuilt
Grove Street, and many trees, shrubs, and flowers. They were
active in a staggering number of civic clubs, including the
Men's Club, Progressive Club, Mother's Club, Garden Club,
Golf Club, and the Peterborough Board of Trade. They also
served as trustees and directors of two local banks. Taken as a
whole it seems almost like a European model of charity, the
local royalty dispensing favors on the countryside.

Mary Lyons Cheney Schofield, another Associate, was a
leading benefactor. A wealthy heiress with a regal bearing and
an "iron will," Schofield funded projects on a grand scale that
went beyond her fellow Associates. She hired Ralph Adams
Cram to design a Gothic Episcopal church in Peterborough.
Cram was nationally famous for his work at West Point and the
world's largest Gothic-style church, the Episcopal Cathedral
of St. John the Divine. He lectured widely, proselytizing for
Gothic architecture. Cram believed in Gothic architecture as
a moral force to restore Christianity and reform society. (In the
1920s he was the only architect on the cover of *Time* magazine;
Frank Lloyd Wright followed twelve years later.) Schofield also
bought the site of another Peterborough mill, the Old Bell
Mill, which had burned down. She had an architect design a
villa like those she had enjoyed in the South of France. She
called her riverside retreat "Beside Still Waters" and its adjoining Italian-style garden "Waterfall Terrace." To improve her
view, she conducted her own private urban renewal project,
replacing a poor neighborhood with Mediterranean villas. (It

was Schofield who had found the Grove Street tenements objectionable.) When a carter persisted in working on Sundays across from her new church, she would cross the street to scold him, insisting that he close the barn doors. She solved the "problem" by buying the barn.

Schofield was "ubiquitous," as one town history said. She started the first nursery school north of Boston and sent her chauffeur to pick up the children. She set up training on her estate for women farmers ("Farmerettes"), as part of the National Women's Land Army to feed the homefront in World War I, and organized a club to support soldiers in World War II. She saw to it that unmarried women teachers were housed in "The Manse," and she hosted teas there. At one tea she had offered a handsome gift to the town to build a new school where she thought it belonged. Her guests declined the offer. "Well then, you build your school," she said.

The editor of the *Peterborough Transcript* welcomed her improvements. If "the community is clean, progressive, with a fine sense of civic pride, we are apt to be happy and progressive ourselves."

The Associates were creating a high-minded culture—the "higher civilization" that former Governor Bass had called for, moving to the "higher level" that Russell had spoken of when dedicating the Town House. They were joined by the arrival of summer arts camps, a neighborhood of high culture in the fresh air. Abandoned farms made good homes for summer theaters. They were a part of New Hampshire's boom in summer camps in an era that believed in the power of the outdoors to rescue children from the crowded city. "The children, with their pale faces, feeble digestion, and underdeveloped bodies, are beginning to show the effects of this unwholesome way of living," said the 1923 booklet for the Sargent Camp for Girls in Peterborough. "The cry is, back to the country and its fresh air, its green fields, pure water and shady woods."

The Out-Door Players set up on forty acres about two miles north of the village in 1914. The land had a natural amphitheater, which was used "for instruction in the arranging of plays, pantomimes, pageants and interpretative dancing." Students were advised to come prepared "for life in the great outdoors." The camp was run by Marie Ware Laughton, "student of Pantomime and the Drama in Paris and London." She had on staff the "Ballet Master and Director Choreographic; of the First Imperial Russian Ballet School in America" who taught "Russian interpretative dancing" and "Character dancing: Greek, Oriental, Hungarian, Pastoral and others of like character."

"Now, in the midst of war, is the time to prepare for Peace," said the booklet announcing the 1918 summer season. "We have caught the wrong spirit of war-time co-operation if we are not preparing to hold up America's high standard in Art and realizing that we are doing our part if we help to brighten life by clean entertainment." The booklet was illustrated with scenes from the previous summer's pageant, "The Torch Bearers," showing Joan of Arc in one photo, and Egyptians in another.

Next to the Out-Door Players, Mariarden opened in 1922. The name was a combination of the founder's first name and the forest west of Stratford-upon-Avon that was the setting for Shakespeare's *As You Like It*. Marie Currier had trained as a Shakespearean actress under Edwin Booth and played Ophelia in Hamlet. After several years on the Boston stage, she married Guy Currier, a lawyer and financier who had backed Joseph P. Kennedy's takeover of the RKO film company. His close friend Calvin Coolidge had wanted him to serve as vice president. The Curriers owned a number of farms in Peterborough. Marie had bought the first one on a whim at an auction. Near the farm they finally chose as their summer home, Guy had an eighteen-hole golf course built. (In the winters they lived in Boston, or in a villa in Florence.) She bought another farm for the Mariarden. On 150 acres she had Boston architects design forty buildings for rehearsals, sleeping, and dining. The main stage was a Shakespearean set built by a leading set designer in Boston and trucked in pieces to New Hampshire. The stage was in a six-hundred-seat natural amphitheater. (There's a wonderful photo of an actress cocooned in mosquito netting.)

Shakespearean drama and modern dance were taught at Mariarden, which is believed to be the first professional outdoor theater in America. Mariarden was the New England home for the Denishawn dancers, Ruth St. Denis and Ted Shawn, the top modern dancers of the 1920s. Martha Graham had started out with the Denishawn school in Los Angeles and traveled east as a leading soloist, dancing in New York and at Mariarden. Paul Robeson played in Eugene O'Neill's *The Emperor Jones.* Bette Davis began at Mariarden. Her mother had brought her to Peterborough, but she could not afford the tuition at Mariarden, so she enrolled her daughter at the Out-Door Players. Davis was discovered dancing there and given a full scholarship to Mariarden. She performed in *As You Like It, A Midsummer's Night Dream,* and many dance productions.

Art begat art. Another summer theater, the Peterborough Players, began up the road. Edith Bond Stearns, daughter of a successful Boston businessman, stayed at Mariarden before buying an old farm and starting a theater in the barn. "It is the aim of Our Playhouse to present dramas of poetic quality whether in verse or prose in full recognition of the theatrical harmonies uniting speech, poetry, music, the dance and scenic design. Our Playhouse is presenting neglected classics, the best available contemporary drama and hopes also to encourage the young playwrights of the future," Stearns said in 1933. The first play was an experimental "poem/play with musical accompaniment," *Manikin and Minikin,* by a writer-in-residence at the MacDowell Colony, a retreat for writers, artists, and composers. The Colony was adjacent to the Out-Door Players and Mariarden.

The MacDowell Colony, founded in 1907, was sustained by the tireless devotion of Marian MacDowell after the death of her husband, the composer Edward MacDowell. They, too, had come to Peterborough and bought an old farm, and in time decided to build studios in the woods where artists could work. To raise money and spread the Colony's name, Marian staged a series of pageants, one act plays, and music in an outdoor amphitheater, which drew people to Peterborough. She also barnstormed the country, giving piano recitals to raise money until she was seventy-six years old.

Marian MacDowell, and the many artists who came to the Colony, made Peterborough well known. But it was one colonist who bestowed upon Peterborough an identity that has become its logo. Thornton Wilder wrote *Our Town* in 1937, drawing on his observations of Peterborough and a half-dozen other New Hampshire towns. Grove Street is believed to have inspired the name of Grover's Corners, the town in the play. With *Our Town,* Peterborough ascended to that rarefied place where people confuse fiction and life, mistaking one for another. For some, Peterborough *is Our Town.* (A few years ago, a *Boston Globe* reporter asked a local newspaper publisher if Thornton Wilder still lives there.)

The summer arts camps and the Colonial Revival makeover fused to create the Blueblood Milltown. This is a town that has cultural aspirations far beyond the usual chamber of commerce sidewalk sales and dinner theater with a production of *The Odd Couple.* In 1923 two tourists told a local newspaper reporter that they were surprised at "the intelligence of the community, the atmosphere being of culture and refinement."

As grand as it is to be exalted by gifts, by this summer person's culture of improvement and rural uplift, it can be a little irritating living in someone else's hobby. A model train layout is a fun thing to examine, but you wouldn't want to live in Plasticville.

In 1921 the Associates tore down the other big mill downtown, the Old Shoe Factory, also known as the Old Basket Shop. Unlike the Phoenix Mill, this five-story wooden mill had been continuously occupied since 1900 and housed a basket company. They moved the company to a new factory they built away from the central village and removed what they considered to be an eyesore. Schofield bought the land, filled in the foundation, and planted shrubs.

The Associates had different plans for the Phoenix Mill. They offered to donate it to the town to be used as a high school with a new addition for a gym paid for by Schofield.

This gift got a cool reception. Many people believed that the Associates were driving industry out of town: they had refused good offers for the Phoenix Mill, and they had torn down the Old Shoe Factory.

These objections surprised the Associates, and they hesitated to respond. Russell, who had spoken to the school board, "did not believe it fitting to argue upon the value of the proposed gift." They were not against industry in the right place. It was not their intention that Peterborough become "only a beautiful town to look upon with nothing vital about it," Russell had said, dedicating the Town House. "We want new workers in Peterborough, but we want our Town House, our town and its institutions to make them know the power and inspiration of a progressive community and a true democracy."

The town refused the gift, voting it down at a meeting. The following year the Associates leveled the Old Phoenix Mill. With the fall of the mill, the Associates' reforms were waning, and by the end of the 1920s they had ceased. The Associates were getting old. Mary Schofield moved to Quebec, where she spent her last days. Russell rarely came to Peterborough any more. His wife had taken ill, and they stayed at their Nantucket estate. Clara Bass died in 1933, and Robert Bass was occupied with national issues.

The Associates had removed the town's two largest buildings, changing the industrial profile of a milltown to one of a village. The spire of the Unitarian church and the cupola of the Town House were now the town's signature. There was no mistaking Peterborough for some small version of Lowell.

"The Associates' intention appears to have been to create a Utopian community of farmers, summer residents, blue-collar immigrants, and professionals. They attempted to transform Peterborough into a town of alluring, glory-producing landscapes," concludes geographer Scott Roper.

The whiff of Utopia hangs over Peterborough. Utopia is the good place that is nowhere. It's a promise, a polemic, a program. In most Utopias the contradictions of the human heart are disciplined by a central authority. One idea, one belief. Utopias are hobbies run amuck, a whim that can become a straitjacket.

No utopia succeeds. Peterborough isn't one idea, but rather the collision of two ideas. The summer person's utopia, the Republic of Old Money, rubs up against the granite practicality of New Hampshire, creating the tectonics of this place. In recent years Peterborough's residents have argued, at times contentiously, about whether to allow a McDonald's, to rezone to build a third shopping center, to expand or revoke a proposed industrial park, to declare a one-year moratorium for building permits, to pave a riverside bike path, and to allow an abstract (or erotic, depending on what you saw) sculpture in a public park. Many of these debates were drawn on the lines that can be found in the Associates' vision: beautify town and welcome industry.

The sign coming into town still holds. The sign is still the flag of the town, the alpha and the omega of all debates. Welcome to Peterborough. A good town to live in. But how do we define that? And who gets to decide? You have one hour for the exam. Use both sides of the page in the blue book. Or you have a lifetime, your only lifetime, and the only land we have been given, to build a good town. Ready? Begin.

Big Changes

in Small Places

One House

Private houses lead private, untold lives. The history of the private house is one of hearsay and conjecture. We know very little about our own home. We may know the year it was built or thereabouts; we may have seen an old photo or two of the place with different trees and flowers, or heard a story about our house from a neighbor. If we live in an old New England house, we may be living in the "Adams" or "Prescott" house, even though the last Adams or Prescott to live there was buried long ago. But the family pedigree of a house is only the barest outline.

Houses are taciturn. "You could look it up," Casey Stengel said, referring to the record book. You can't do that with the common house; its history is unwritten.

We mistake this reticence for stasis. We think that not much has gone on with these walls. We think of the home as the place of constancy. We return home to our own set scene, our little domestic diorama, as contrived (and flimsy) as those shoebox dioramas you may have made in grade school. But the history of most houses is one of change.

Even a relatively new house is a do-it-yourself work in progress. Wander the aisles of Home Depot if you want to see this domestic ambition. Each day a river of building materials flows out of these warehouse stores, new floors, walls, roofs, windows, bathrooms, lighting . . . There is little beyond the cement slab or basement that a homeowner will not change. A few years ago preservationists wanted to study a few unchanged Levitt houses. Starting in 1947, there were more than 17,000 houses built in Levittown, New York. They could not find one unchanged.

The history of our house is typical, and I will tell it as we learned it. Our house is modest, built perhaps in the 1880s, with its gable end close to the road. (Very close: The house is twenty-two feet wide and exactly twenty-two feet from the road. I had to pace it off when a zoning question came up.) It's a plain "high-post cape." I think of it as the Greek Revival after it had been down on the farm for fifty years or more. The language of the Greek Revival remains in the corner pilasters, but the builders did not vary one inch from building basic shelter. This classical vernacular is a dress code that corresponds to the respect Americans paid to classical Greece and Rome. Anyone with some book-learning knew the poets and historians of the classics. In common use this later Greek Revival created the trim, spare white houses that became the calendar cheesecake of the tourist bureau.

Around here we take great pride in the eighteenth-century Georgians and capes, and the early nineteenth-century brick Federal houses. Houses like ours are overlooked. Real-estate agents list them as a generic "New Englander" or "New England Villager." (They lack the knowledge, but then so do their clients. We are blind; our contemporary landscape is built by the blind for the blind.)

The house, barn, and outbuildings are on eight acres of

old-field pasture and woods bordering a brook. Some great old trees shelter the house—a silver maple, a large ash, aging sugar maples, pines, and tamaracks, which are more common to the north. Someone loved those tamaracks, perhaps the same person who planted the lilacs, phlox, and hostas. They are hardy plants that bore many gardeners; we never tire of looking at them. In the pasture are two elderly apple trees, which we keep pruned. They still fruit, some years magnificently. When our neighbor's horses are standing under the trees at apple blossom time, I feel rich. Enough scene setting; it's misleading. This sounds like a Wallace Nutting country scene—the quiet and repose of "bygone" days. The story is otherwise.

Adjoining the main house is an ell, a later addition in the tradition of New England's connected farm houses, a unique lineup of farmhouse, kitchen building, storage shed, and barn, known by the nineteenth-century children's verse: "big house, little house, back house, barn." The back part of the ell was once a summer porch, we were told. It was likely built after the barn was moved from where it joined the front of the ell. Here we are coming to the heart of our story.

On the south side of the house, right by the part of the ell that was once a summer porch, is a wonderful sunken garden we call, with mock-formality, "the grotto." (In the nineteenth century, picturesque landscapers like Frederick Law Olmsted or Calvert Vaux would sometimes include a grotto for contemplation of the "sublime.") The silver maple shades this fine outdoor room, and the hostas bloom in front of a stone wall.

This is where the barn used to be—that's the first thing we learned from the previous homeowners. The stone wall was part of the barn's foundation. At some point—when?—the barn was detached from the house and dragged downhill and out back where it sits today. There are some telltale cut boards that reveal where the house's roof may have met the barn wall.

With the barn removed, the front of the ell was extended about six feet to create a small porch and entrance for the summer porch, which was added at the same time. This, at least, is my theory.

The authors of this later work lacked the skills of the first builders. The added six feet droops off the side, giving it a hang-dog look, and the construction on the ex-summer porch is too light. Maybe they thought of the porch as temporary.

Why did they move the barn? Did it mark a change in farming practices? Was it for fashion or necessity?

The barn offers another clue to the changes on these few acres. Old Yankees used to clapboard only the public sides of their connected barns—the front and maybe a side facing a road. The other walls would be left in boards. Think of dressing for church, but wearing a tie and jacket on your front—since that is what the minister will see—and dirty overalls on your back.

On our barn the clapboards are weathered brown, and some are curling off, but there was one odd thing: why was the side, which now faced the brook, clapboarded? When I pictured the barn pulled up alongside the house, that clapboarded side only faced trees, the pasture, and a good ways off, the Bennington Road, a state route.

I mentioned this to a neighbor, who said: Oh, didn't you know? The road used to run diagonally across the pasture. And that road at the time was the major north-south route, the road to the state capital [grandly titled the Contoocook Valley Highway]. You can be sure that your barn would be properly dressed to face a public thoroughfare.

If I look carefully, particularly on a day with a dusting of early snow, I can make out the ghost of this old road, attended by the boulders that were once removed from its right of way.

Let us return to that pasture scene with the horses grazing under the apple trees in blossom. On the other side of the fence is the silver maple, and tamaracks shading the white house, and the old brown barn with a fading red door. A nice scene. But what looks settled is really another American landscape—house, barn, and road—on the move.

Moving buildings was common. In my town a quick, incomplete survey around the common and the main street comes up with many moved buildings. The Meetinghouse was built in 1820 and moved back about seventy-five feet in 1851. A lower floor was added inside. Across the common, the Baptist Literary and Scientific Institute was built in 1836; it was moved in 1893, turned to face the common and given an addition called by one resident, "a nose." This building served as Hancock's school for more than a hundred years. It was recently remodeled— "nose" and all—for use as town offices. Down the street, the Whitcomb store was moved sometime after 1898 around the corner to be a barbershop and a pool room. Today it's a house. Next door, the library has received two additions, one in front in 1925 and one out back in 1988, for which a house was moved up the main street. This is a small fraction of the many houses and barns that have been moved, most pulled on rolling logs or wooden wheels by teams of oxen and horses.

"The frequency of moving major domestic and agricultural buildings in eighteenth and nineteenth century New England is staggering," writes architect Thomas C. Hubka in *Big House, Little House, Back House, Barn*. "When the history of building movement in a particular New England town is accurately recorded . . . it appears as if the entire town was constantly being moved about."

One Flight Up

The second floor of the Granite Block creaks with each step you take. The hall rolls and dips, a sea swell of maple planks. It seems like a visual distortion at first, a migraine coming on. You want to reach for a hand railing. The second floor is a fusty place, up steep stairs, with high ceilings and doors with transoms, the kind of place used as a setting for film noir detective movies. The Granite Block was built in 1847 and burned in 1902. It began as a two-and-a-half story granite building with a steeply pitched roof. After the fire, it rose with two more wooden stories and an addition, which were covered in stucco. The addition, about twenty feet on the south side, may have been poorly built. The bulge in the floor marks where 1847 joins 1902.

This is an appropriate monument to nineteenth century America. The America of the 1840s was a small country of farmers, but 1900s America was an industrial colossus, an empire on the make. The America of the 1840s never fit well with 1900s America. This was the lament of so many writers, reformers, and preachers. They had grown up barefoot in country villages; by middle age they were strangers in their own land. New Hampshire was in many ways a smaller place by the turn of the century, but like the rest of America it did its best to puff itself up with the gospel of busyness.

The wooden addition may have been lightly framed or never had a proper foundation. It is also sitting on the lip of a hidden canal. This has made for a rocky marriage: while 1847 is settled in its granite sureness, 1902 wants to dance. The addition may be sinking, and a few years ago the stucco was sheering off one side. (Vinyl siding buttoned it back up for another generation.)

The Granite Block has that most coveted quality in real estate: "location." It is at the heart of Peterborough, New Hampshire, corner of Main and Grove Streets, once the premier spot for seeing and being seen, known through the years as Robbe's, Cass's, Trufant's, and Bishop's Corner.

Architect Rick Monahon has his office on the second floor. Monahon likes being across from the town offices, where he can see who's coming and going from the planning board. This kind of peripheral intelligence is invaluable and gives small-town life that touch of the panopticon. ("Guess who I saw today coming out of the drugstore with a quart bottle of Pepto Bismol?")

There are seven other tenants on the second floor: artists, an editor, a graphic designer, a real-estate inspector, and an international salt broker. ("Quality salt sales.") In the 1950s and 1960s there was a lawyer, an insurance agent, Lesley King's Beauty Shop, and Dr. Karl S. Keyes, Peterborough's first full-time dentist. Dr. Keyes had his office on the second floor from 1899 to 1961. Another dentist took his place for a dozen years. Every so often Monahan will find someone roaming the hall who will ask him, "Say, wasn't there a dentist up here?" Boy, he thinks, have you been putting things off.

The third floor is a ruin. Big sections of the plaster ceiling have fallen. The ceiling looks like a map of some ancient world, with islands of remaining plaster surrounded by the exposed wooden laths. Plaster dust crunches underfoot. This beautiful, ruined room has even higher ceilings than the second floor, and two long rows of old windows with wavy glass looking out on Main and Grove Streets. Anywhere else this would be prime loft space. Here it acts like many old barns—it's a magnet for the half-thrown-out: Monahan's filed architectural drawings and those of other architects for the last thirty years, dead computers, boxes and trunks, the retail furnishings from Cass's (later Trufant's) men's clothing shop, and uniforms and targets from when this was a drill hall for the National Guard. This floor shares a fire wall with the unused upper two stories of the adjoining Steele's building.

The upper stories have fallen into that limbo known as being "out of code": they need another set of stairs, fire sprinklers, and perhaps an elevator. The low rent for this space would not immediately pay for these improvements. The "code" is the name of the ghost who walks these vacant floors. Our best intentions to protect life and property from fire, to insist that all citizens, whether disabled or "temporarily able-bodied" can go where they choose, have leveled the upper stories.

Looking out on the street you have that odd feeling of spying on the present from the past. In these cast-off spaces it seems as if time itself had settled like plaster dust.

Thirty years ago J. B. Jackson, a pioneering observer of the American landscape, looked above the storefronts on Main Street and noticed that the upper stories were being deserted. "Each year I see a few more windows dark and uncared for, even obliterated by commercial facades. Despite all the activity on the street floor, the second and third and fourth floors of the older brick buildings are no longer in demand. Not many years ago they accommodated the offices of lawyers and dentists and doctors; dance studios and certified public accountants. Now the gold lettering has vanished from the windows, and even the street door leading to the stairs is blocked. Sooner or later the buildings themselves will be torn down, to be replaced by one-story buildings or parking lots."

The ghost town upstairs is a part of America's "love of horizontal spaces," Jackson said. Big houses with the best address in town—wide porches under old trees—had been forsaken, traded in for the new horizontal model, the suburban ranch house. Old multi-storied mills were abandoned as businesses built the modern all-on-one-level space they required. The modern farm, too, he noted, organized work with a horizontal layout, the old barn and silo replaced with a one-story cement block building and a trench silo.

"Everywhere the tendency to eliminate the vertical is evident," Jackson said. "Increased mobility, and even more, an increased experience of uninterrupted speed—whether on the highway or the ski slope or on the surface of the water—bring with them a sharpened awareness of horizontal space." Even the skyscraper, he believed, was "essentially a stack of large, uninterrupted horizontal spaces."

After World War II, the new America was one story—ranch house, elementary school, shopping center. Some old buildings had their tops loped off; the upper floors of hotels and opera houses were torn down. The facades of the remaining stump were scrubbed of ornament, and the first floor was reborn as a twin to the new shopping center. Modern and sleek if you're the architect; faceless and sterile if you've inherited the building forty years later. Face-lifts don't age well.

Some of the remaining upper floors were blocked off and forgotten. They have fallen off the map, like people who have given up looking for work. They are unemployed, but they are not counted in the unemployment statistics. This is vacant space that may not be counted in the vacancy rates. In his wonderful short story, *In the Heart of the Heart of the Country*, William Gass wrote of the empty storefronts in a small Indiana town: "What do the sightless windows see, I wonder, when the sun throws a passerby against them? Here a stair unfolds toward the street—dark, rickety, and treacherous—and I always feel, as I pass it, that if I just went carefully up and turned the corner at the landing, I would find myself out of the world. But I've never had the courage."

I asked a real-estate agent, who had thirty years experience in a small New England city, about leasing upper floors. "No one comes in looking for second-floor space," he said. "There has been some second- and third-floor space that's literally been available for years. Thirty years ago a lot of doctors and lawyers occupied the second floor. Over the years it's fallen on hard times—unless you have an elevator. There are a number of buildings downtown, their upper floors are shut off. It's economically unfeasible to bring it up to code. All it's doing is acting as a roof."

The second floor of Main Street was a lost America, or so it seemed until I asked around some more. A second real-estate agent in the same city contradicted everything the first man had said. There was a strong desire for second-floor space. He had converted many offices to apartments. He had ninety apartments, but he could rent them three times over. I asked him about the back half of a building that had never recovered from a fire in the 1940s. The third floor was closed off. It needed a second exit, fire sprinklers. He could bring it up to code and get his money back, he said.

The dust has begun to shift in the ghost town upstairs. Urban planners love the second floor. They promote it in their papers and conferences under the headings of "mixed-use," "diversity," "integration," and "infill." Second floors are good, they say. When people live downtown, the town thrives, incomes and expectations mix, and less countryside is consumed by new mini-fiefdoms. Vermont has recently passed a law to encourage the restoration of upper stories, in part with tax incentives. The ghost town upstairs has haunted our Main Streets. Without that life one story up, many towns withered.

I had expected a story of loss. This revival is surprising, but it fits the usual American story of changes in the land: the way we light out for the territory, and come ricocheting back. We head west, south, to suburbs, exurbs, edge cities, big open places. Lonely, we pull up stakes and head back to the city, rediscover small towns, old city neighborhoods, street-car suburbs, or even post-war Levittowns. It's less a pattern of settlement than a jitterbug.

Consider the history of one building, 23 Church Street in Burlington, Vermont. It was built about 1875 as a creamery. Sometime in the 1920s, the one-story creamery was jacked up, and two stories were built underneath. Church Street had become a thriving commercial district. The new first floor of the ex-creamery was at various times a grocery and a paint store. The upper two stories last served as an apartment in 1946 — that is the date of the newspapers lining the shelves. Then, in keeping with postwar horizontal America, the upper floors were abandoned. Now, fifty-five years later, the old creamery building apartments are being renovated, aided by a grant from a downtown reinvestment fund. Built, changed, abandoned, reclaimed. That's our hometowns — reinvented every generation.

One Tree

For years I have kept watch over some large trees nearby, great oaks and ashes, surviving majestic elms. I have seen some of these great trees die, while others may be as nearly invisible as a living thing can be. I am an unofficial tree warden until such time as we appoint one to make house calls, as the French do for the mothers of newborns.

I wonder about some of these trees, like the great oak by an abandoned dirt road. Surely, many trees near it were felled, but this oak was spared by men who needed the wood. Why? Was it because of an old-country reverence for oaks by the Scotch-Irish settlers? There is no way of knowing.

I have stopped and knocked at the door of the house shaded by that tree: Excuse me, I've been admiring your oak for years . . . Once they get past the oddity — ("What does he want?" "He says he's here about our tree.") — they say they like the oak. Their father used to sit under it every day. They know nothing more about it. In fact, no one ever knows anything about these graceful old trees, except that they are old. How old? They don't know.

I have wanted to linger and look at some of the big trees that I pass, but that would be suspicious. A guy lurking by your house who says he's looking at your ash is headed for a listing in the police log. So I convinced a friend and photographer, Jim Howard, to come along. Jim is a trained negotiator who is hired by international companies to try and set things right. He worked at a hotel in Asia run by a European company where there were a dozen nationalities on staff, and a multiplicity of distrust. The Japanese had problems with the Chinese, the Germans with the French, but everyone was united in hating the Americans. I knew that if we were confronted by an angry land owner, Jim would calm things down.

With a photographer, I was legitimate. I could loiter for hours. What we were doing was odd, but at least visible. When we were photographing an elm that rose like green fireworks out of a backyard, a neighbor came over to ask us what we were doing. I told him. "Quite a tree, isn't it?" I asked him. "That thing?—*That's* what you're taking pictures of?" He squinted at the tree, as if checking to see if it had moved, squinted at me, at Jim, and walked away.

One of my favorite trees is an elm by a stone arch bridge in Hillsborough, New Hampshire. This is the most changed landscape within twenty miles of where I live. The narrow, two-lane, stone arch bridge carried the major north-south route until just several years ago. A new bridge was built, and a new road cut through to meet up with a large new highway bypass. A MacDonald's and a Rite-Aid Drugstore sprouted, and the whole thing is now a chunk of everywhere/nowhere America.

The elm stands right at the edge of Hillsboro Ford. Its closest neighbors are an eight-story-tall Ford sign, and, since the attack of 9/11, an immense American flag, thirty by sixty feet, making it eighteen hundred square feet, the footprint of a good-sized house. The Ford dealership is a replica of Mount Vernon—if Mount Vernon had a bright blue steel roof and rows of new pick-up trucks parked in front. This is quite the scene: new bridge, closed stone arch bridge, elm, Ford sign, flag, rows of shiny trucks, and Mount Vernon. There is paving on both sides of the river. I have seen a photo of the old bridge around 1900; this was a tranquil country crossing.

With Jim along, I am able to spend hours looking around, wandering the lot with immunity from the car salesmen. (I'd like to trade in this landscape, trade in this sprawl, for something greener.)

The elm is parked in a narrow spot: eight feet from a small marker for the state right-of-way and the old road, ten feet from the new trucks. Looking toward the new bridge from the tree, the view is all telephone poles and wires and street lights and guardrails and cars. I amble down the riverbank and look back up toward the tree. It's a sea wall of truck grills parked on top of a wall of big rocks. This mesa has been built up from what was likely once wetland. The waters bend in an oxbow here, with the dealership in the middle.

In my travels around the lot, I ask the salesmen I meet what they think of the tree. "That's quite a tree out there," I say. "Yeah, yup, yup," says one, moving away from me. This matches the response of a twenty-something salesman. "Any idea of how old that tree is?" I ask. "It's older than me," he says, satisfied with his answer. Another salesman, an older man, tells me that there is a woman who comes in to check on the tree. "She comes in any time we park a vehicle by it." "I guess that gets annoying," I say. "Well she's right," he says. "It's the last one around. We shouldn't do it. She keeps a good eye on us."

A woman in a glassed-in office calls out to me, "It's got a plaque on it." She's looking at a computer screen of numbers. I go outside and find a discrete brass plaque, about the size of a snapshot, an attempt to lift the tree from invisibility:

HISTORIC ELM
THIS TREE IS HEREBY DESIGNATED
A HISTORIC LANDMARK TO BE
HONORED AND PRESERVED FOR
FUTURE GENERATIONS.

ELM RESEARCH INSTITUTE
HARRISVILLE, N.H.

The elm rises to a height of about a hundred feet, branching from three principal trunks, which keep dividing on the way to the spreading crown. I study how the three trunks each split into two trunks about six feet up, and then divide again about eight feet higher, and so on, a rising fountain spray.

Two guys driving by in a black pickup truck—"Colonial Paving"—see Jim, and one calls out, "Take a picture of me! I'm in a Ford!" I tell him we're taking a picture of the tree. He looks at the tree and the flag. "That's a big hairy flag!" he says.

The general manager comes out to talk with us. He had wanted to come out sooner, but he has a busy showroom and people waiting to talk with him. This is one of the busiest car dealerships I have ever seen. It's good of him to talk to us. Mike Luciano is a short man, a little overweight in his early 40s, and dressed in a white shirt and double-knit pants. He's been at this dealership just three months. His family is still back in Vermont. He goes home on weekends. He's living in an apartment in Peterborough. When I ask him how that is, he tells me that he hasn't lived in an apartment since he was eighteen. He's been a homeowner. He and his family are looking for a house.

Like a good salesman he makes sure to use my first name in his opening sentences. "Well, Howard," he begins. "The ladies from the historic society have talked to me. We used to park vehicles along here. We don't park them here anymore. But this used to be the highway—you're really not going to hurt the roots of the tree by parking here. But, you know, it makes them happy so I do that. We respect the tree. We respect the historic society. It kind of goes along with our—" he stops, and is looking for the word "theme," I think, but he moves on: "We get the big American flag. We're a Ford dealer, so Ford is kinda' like, you know, a millennium-type operation, so we get the big oval up there, you know, started by Henry Ford, and we got the historic tree, so it all kind of goes together. You know, it's our past. We've got more of a Colonial-style operation than most. We have not an all-glass showroom, but more of the look of a Colonial house. It kind of all fits together. And we sell a lot of cars here. We're doing great. We do a lot of community-support type things. And obviously we're kind of patriotic," he says referring to the flag. I ask him for the name of the woman who asks them not to park on the tree. He tells me, and says, "Little old ladies make sure I don't park cars on trees. I'll take the cars away from the tree if it makes them happy."

I hate to think of a world that is not defended by L.O.L. (Little Old Ladies).

I call the L.O.L., Alice Phipps Keach, a minister's widow, as it turns out. I tell her that I'm a writer and I've been looking at that tree, and she takes off, a torrent of words, talking for forty minutes. "The tree is one of the historic wonders of the world," she says, but it's lost "in the middle of the worst architectural mish-mash," of roads and cars and wires.

Alice spoke to the manager just a week after he had arrived. Her car had died, and she ended up at the Ford dealer. She told him that he had a chance for some real civic leadership when he went to introduce himself to the chamber of commerce. There is a plan for a park across the river from the stone arch bridge. Alice told him that he should propose joining the old bridge to a walkway so the elm would be part of the park. She could see an elegant bench encircling the old tree. And then this park should be linked to the other historic stone arch bridges in town and the Franklin Pierce Homestead, with a bike path planted in new elm trees. This trail would have small low-key historic markers.

"Why don't you run with it?" she had said to the manager. "You have a chance to go to the chamber and set the precedent."

This was more than a "little old lady" fussing over a tree. This was visionary. Her presentation had all the elements to make many people shy away: a passion for change, and the demanding task of imagining something new on land you saw every day. It required an appreciation of the ordinary and a belief that grace mattered.

Alice had been in this position before, she told me. For many years she had waged a one-woman campaign to restore a small park in the center of town. She spoke to the chamber of commerce and the many service clubs, like the Lions. She had a model made, at her expense, showing the redesigned park. She had a chilly reception. After one meeting, someone said, "I think we should tear down the old buildings downtown." After another meeting, she overheard someone saying, "Hillsborough is just a blue-collar town. We don't need that fancy stuff." She turned to that person: "Hillsborough is the only town in New Hampshire that's had a president. What's blue-collar about that?" Finally she gave up her project. Five years later, the park was restored.

The tree is not seen. "Would you take your children on a walk to see that tree? You couldn't do it. There's no place to walk. It's a highway culture. It's really about making money and selling asphalt." The corner is dominated by cheap franchises. They depreciate buildings like that in ten years and walk away. "It's a walkaway corner," she says. "And where's the car, the shiny prized new car, in thirty years? It's squashed, garbage. But where's the tree thirty years later? You can't grow another tree like that. The tragedy is that the tree was here before all this. The stone arch bridge is a gift from man. The tree standing next to it is a gift from God."

The elm by Hillsboro Ford is about one hundred feet tall, and as best as I can tell from my nonscientific polling, this tree is almost invisible. A great tree by a river and a bridge could have been a sacred site in the old religion. This one tree could be an axis mundi, a center of the world, a place to contemplate what's real, for the thousands of centerless, anxious souls who speed by each day.

If I said this tree is a shrine, would we look at it? If I said Washington stood here, would we honor it? But it is a tree, one tree among millions (just as we are one among millions), and that is not enough for us. I can point to the plaque on its trunk and tell you that this tree is a victor, a survivor. I can tell you that it is brave—but trees are not brave. I can say that its survival is miraculous—but all trees are miraculous. And at the same time, trees are not victorious survivors or miracles; they just are. But that is never enough for us.

"There is no word in our language that cannot become typical to us of nature by giving it emphasis," Ralph Waldo Emerson wrote in his journal. "The world is a Dancer; it is a Rosary; it is a Torrent; it is a Boat; a Mist; a Spider's Snare; it is what you will; and the metaphor will hold, & it will give the imagination keen pleasure. Swifter than light the World converts itself into that thing you name & all things find their right place under this new & capricious classification. There is no thing small or mean to the soul. It derives as grand a joy from symbolizing the Godhead or his Universe under the form of a moth or a gnat as of a Lord of the Hosts. Must I call the heaven & the earth a maypole & country fair with booths or an anthill or an old coat in order to give you the shock of pleasure which the imagination loves and the sense of spiritual greatness? Call it a blossom, a rod, a wreath of parsley, a tamarisk-crown, a cock, a sparrow, the ear instantly hears & the spirit leaps to the trope."

So—the world is this elm by Hillsboro Ford. The whole world is this one tree. The world is a *Boston Post* Cane, the Washington Elm, a memorial stone placed on a town common, a bobcat track in the mud. Let us make of it what we will. The center is where we find it, if we have courage.

Selected Bibliography

Starting from Paumanok

Foley, Maurice. "Shopping Centers for Long Island." *New York Times,* December 25, 1955.

New York Times. "Center's Covered Mall Designed to Offer Shoppers Protection." April 7, 1962.

———. "Closed-In Malls Aid Retail Sales." May 26, 1963.

———. "Long Island Shops to Face Serpentine Mall." October 7, 1962.

Porterfield, Byron. "Big Garden-Like Mall Dedicated at Huntington Shopping Center." *New York Times,* November 24, 1962.

Whitman, Walt. *Complete Poetry and Collected Prose.* Edited by Justin Kaplan. Library of America, 1982.

Williams, William Carlos. *In the American Grain.* New Direction Books, 1956.

The Walking Stick and the Edge of the Universe

Aldrich, Eric. "Hancock Listens to Stars." *Keene (N.H.) Sentinel,* January 13, 1995.

Allen, Anne Wallace. "Tradition of Boston Post Canes Goes on in New England." *Associated Press,* May 9, 2002.

Clark, Tim. "The Keepers of the Cane." *Yankee,* March 1983.

DuBois, Brendan. "The Boston Post Cane: Circulation 'Gimmick' Now Americana." *Hampton (N.H.) Union,* March 28, 1984.

Eklund, Jane. "Antrim's Boston Post Cane." *Monadnock (N.H.)Ledger,* June 20, 2002.

Epping, N.H., Board of Selectmen. Meeting Minutes, December 4, 2000.

Guadazno, Laurel. "Edwin A. Grozier and the Boston Post." *Provincetown Banner,* January 6, 2000.

———. "The Boston Post Cane." *Provincetown Banner,* January 13, 2000.

National Radio Astronomy Observatory Web site, http://www.nrao.edu.

Nolin, Lori A. "Dennis Preserves Aging Tradition." *Cape Cod Times,* August 11, 2000.

Peterborough Transcript. "Greenville Post Cane Awarded: Those Were the Days . . .", February 4, 1993.

Schreider, Jason. "Boston Post Cane: For More than 90 Years, Towns have Honored Eldest." *The Union Leader,* May 3, 2002.

Staples, Barbara. *The Granite State's Boston Post Cane: A New England Tradition.* Flemming Press, 1999.

The Washington Elm Reassembled

Axelrod, Alan, ed. *The Colonial Revival in America.* Norton, 1985.

Batchelder, Samuel Francis. "The Washington Elm Tradition . . . Is it True?" Reprinted from the *Cambridge Tribune,* 1925.

Batchelder Collection, Samuel Francis. Cambridge Historical Society.

———. "The Washington Elm Tradition." *Proceedings for the Years 1923 and 1924.* Publications XVII, the Cambridge Historical Society, 1931.

Boorstin, Daniel J. *The Americans: The National Experience.* Vintage Books, 1965.

Brown, Abbie Farwell. "Notable Trees About Boston." *New England Magazine,* July 1900.

Bruner, Erika S. "Historical Footnote." *Cambridge Chronicle,* November 4, 1993.

Cambridge City Council. *Cambridge in the Centennial. Proceedings, July 3, 1875 . . .* John Wilson & Son, 1875.

Cambridge Historical Commission. Washington Elm file.

Campanella, Thomas J. *Republic of Shade: New England and the American Elm.* Yale University Press, 2003.

Connor, Sheila. *New England Natives.* Harvard University Press, 1994.

Cutter, Watson Grant. *Family Traditions Concerning the Washington Elm.* Cambridge, Mass., 1907.

Dame, L. L. "Historic Trees: The Washington Elm; The Eliot Oak." *Bay State Monthly,* February 1884.

Dowden, Ken. *European Paganism.* Routledge, 2000.

Durkheim, Emile. *The Elementary Forms of the Religious Life.* 1915. Reprint, Free Press, 1965.

Fleming, Ronald Lee, and Lauri A. Halderman. *On Common Ground: Caring for Shared Land from Town Common to Urban Park.* Harvard Common Press, 1982.

Flexner, James Thomas. *George Washington in the American Revolution (1775-1783).* Little, Brown, 1967.

Frazer, James George. *The Golden Bough.* Macmillan, 1951.

Ellis, Peter Berresford. *The Druids.* Eerdmans, 1994.

George Washington Bicentennial Commission. *History of the George Washington Bicentennial Celebration . . . Literature Series.* 3 vols. 1932.

Gilman, Arthur, ed. *Theatrum Majorum . . . The Diary of Dorothy Dudley.* 1875. Reprint, New York Times & Arno Press, 1971.

Hannah Winthrop Chapter of the National Society of the Daughters of the American Revolution. *An Historic Guide to Cambridge.* Cambridge, 1907.

Holmes, Oliver Wendell. *The Works of Oliver Wendell Holmes,* vol. 3, *The Poet at the Breakfast Table.* Houghton Mifflin, 1896.

Hornblower, Simon, and Anthony Spawforth, eds. *The Oxford Companion to Classical Civilization.* Oxford University Press, 1998.

Hutchins, Catherine E., ed. *Everyday Life in the Early Republic.* Henry Francis duPont Winterthur Museum, 1994.

Kammen, Michael. *Mystic Chords of Memory.* Knopf, 1991.

Kelley, Klara Bonsack, and Harris Francis. *Navajo Sacred Places.* Indiana University Press, 1994.

Lambert, Henry. "Forests and Forestry in Europe and America." *New England Magazine,* July 1893.

Levy, Jerrold E. *In the Beginning: The Navajo Genesis.* University of California Press, 1998.

Linford, Laurence D. *Navajo Places.* University of Utah Press, 2000.

Longfellow, Henry Wadsworth. *The Complete Poetical Works of Henry Wadsworth Longfellow*. Houghton Mifflin, 1893.

Lowell, James Russell. *The Complete Poetical Works of James Russell Lowell*. Houghton Mifflin, 1897.

Marling, Karal Ann. *George Washington Slept Here*. Harvard University Press, 1988.

Martyn, Charles. *The Life of Artemas Ward*. 1921. Reprint, Kennikat Press, 1970.

McKenzie, Alexander. "Washington in Cambridge." *Atlantic Monthly*, July 1875.

Milosz, Czeslaw, ed. *A Book of Luminous Things: An International Anthology of Poetry*. Harcourt Brace, 1996.

Park Commissioners Report, 1927, 1931, 1932. Cambridge, Mass.

Richens, R. H. *Elm*. Cambridge University Press, 1983.

Schauffler, Richard Haven. *Washington's Birthday*. 1910. Reprint, Dodd, Mead, 1950.

Schwartz, Barry. *George Washington: The Making of an American Symbol*. Free Press, 1987.

Society for the Preservation of New England Antiquities. *Old Time New England*. "The Washington Elm, Cambridge." January 1924.

Truettner, William H., and Roger B. Stein, eds. *Picturing Old New England*. Yale University Press, 1999.

Weems, Mason Locke. *The Life of Washington*. Edited by Marcus Cunliffe. Belknap Press of Harvard University Press, 1962.

Wills, Gary. *Cincinnatus: George Washington and the Enlightenment*. Doubleday, 1984.

Zolbrod, Paul G. *Dine bahane: The Navajo Creation Story*. University of New Mexico Press, 1984.

The Bones of the Earth

Alberti, Leon Battista. *On the Art of Building in Ten Books*. Translated by Joseph Rykwert et al. MIT Press, 1988.

American Society of Civil Engineers, New Hampshire Section. *Five Stone Arch Bridges. Hillsborough, N.H.* (draft). 2000.

Beane, Wendell C., and William G. Doty, eds. *Myths, Rites, Symbols: A Mircea Eliade Reader*. 2 vols. Harper & Row, 1975.

Childs, John W. "Hillsboro's Old Landmark Retained by Bridge Repairs." *New Hampshire Highways Monthly Bulletin*. November-December 1925.

Eklund, Jane. "Enigma in Gold." *Monadnock (N.H.) Ledger.* August 29, 2002.

Family Profile: Taking Care of the Old Man. Video. Accompany (N.H.), 1996.

Franconia Notch Papers. Society for the Protection of New Hampshire Forests archive. University of New Hampshire, n.d.

Gardner, Kevin. *The Granite Kiss: Traditions and Techniques of Building New England Stone Walls.* Countryman Press, 2001.

Garvin, James L. "Notes on the Origins of Arched Stone Bridges in the Contoocook River Valley of New Hampshire." Unpublished, February 23, 2002.

Hancock, Frances Ann Johnson. *Saving the Great Stone Face.* Phoenix Publishing, 1984.

Jones, Kristin, and Andrew Ginzel Web site, http://www.jonesginzel .com.

Knight, Charles Brigham. *The Development of the Town of Roxbury, N.H. and its Schools.* Master's Thesis. Boston University, 1933.

New Hampshire Department of Transportation. "Bridge Maintenance Crew Rebuilds Twin-Arch Stone Bridge in Hillsborough." *On the Move (N.H.),* Winter 2002.

New Hampshire Division of Historical Resources. "Documents Relating to Efforts to Preserve the Great Stone Face or 'Old Man of the Mountain.'" n.d.

Nims Family Papers, 1834-1907. New Hampshire Historical Society.

Suddaby, Elizabeth C. *Nims Family: Seven Generations . . .* Southern Historical Press, 1990.

Thorson, Robert M. *Stone by Stone: The Magnificent History in New England's Stone Walls.* Walker, 2002.

Union Leader (N.H.). "The Old Man Remembered." May 9, 2003.

The Grief Police

ACLU-Florida 2000-2001 Legal Docket, *Warner v. City of Boca Raton,* September 2001.

Albrecht, Eric. "Cemetery Rules Upset One Family." *Columbus (Ohio) Dispatch,* June 20, 2001.

Aries, Philipp. *The Hour of Our Death.* Knopf, 1981.

Emerson, Bo. "Memorials Sprout Alongside Roads, Pose Safety Concerns." *Cox News Service,* August 23, 2002.

Farrell, James J. *Inventing the American Way of Death, 1830-1920.* Temple University Press, 1980.

Hitt, Jack. "The American Way of Death Becomes America's Way of Life." *New York Times,* August 8, 2002.

Jackson, Charles O., ed. *Passing: The Vision of Death in America.* Greenwood Press, 1977.

Jackson, Kenneth T., and Camilo Jose Vergara. *Silent Cities: The Evolution of the American Cemetery.* Princeton Architectural Press, 1989.

Linden-Ward, Blanche. *Silent City on a Hill: Landscapes of Memory and Boston's Mount Auburn Cemetery.* Ohio State University Press, 1989.

Lowenthal, David, and Martyn J. Bowden, eds. *Geographies of the Mind.* Oxford University Press, 1976.

Meyer, Richard E., ed. *Ethnicity in the American Cemetery.* Bowling Green State University Popular Press, 1993.

Reed-Mullins and Associates. *Cemeteries as Open Space Reservations.* U.S. Dept. of Housing and Urban Development, 1970.

"Rules and Regulations for the Cemeteries of the Diocese of Rockville Centre." Diocese of Rockville Centre, n.d.

Sears, John F. *Sacred Places: American Tourist Attractions in the Nineteenth Century.* Oxford University Press, 1989.

Sevigny, Shawna. "Gaudy or Solemn? Debate Rages on." *Keene (N.H.) Sentinel,* May 29, 1997.

Shneidman, Edwin S., ed. *Death: Current Perspectives.* Mayfield Publishing, 1980.

Sloane, David Charles. *The Last Great Necessity: Cemeteries in American History.* Johns Hopkins University Press, 1991.

Stannard, David E., ed. *Death in America.* University of Pennsylvania Press, 1975.

Stilgoe, John R. *Common Landscape of America, 1580 to 1845.* Yale University Press, 1982.

Stowell, Douglas L., et al., "Amended Amicus Curiae Brief of the International Cemetery and Funeral Association in Support of Appellee City of Boca Raton." *Warner v. City of Boca Raton.* 2001.

Testa, Karen. "Judge: Families Not Entitled to Keep Religious Symbols on Graves." *Associated Press,* March 31, 1999.

Standard-Times (Mass.). "Cemetery Flag Rules Upset Vets." June 1, 2002.

Tishler, William H., ed. *Midwestern Landscape Architecture.* University of Illinois Press, 2000.

Winzelberg, David. "Cemetery Bans Mementos of Child Graves." *New York Times,* November 22, 1998.

The Flaneur of the Strip

Adorno, Theodor W., and Walter Benjamin. *The Complete Correspondence.* 1928-1940. Harvard University Press, 1999.

Benjamin, Walter. *The Arcades Project.* Belknap Press of Harvard University Press, 1999.

——. *Illuminations.* Schocken Books, 1969.

——. *Walter Benjamin: Selected Writings.* Vol. 2, 1927-1934. Belknap Press of Harvard University Press, 1996.

Blake, Peter. *God's Own Junkyard.* Holt, Rinehart and Winson, 1964.

Buck-Morss, Susan. *The Dialectics of Seeing: Walter Benjamin and the Arcades Project.* MIT Press, 1991.

Campoli, Julie, and Elizabeth Humstone, Alex Maclean. *Above and Beyond: Visualizing Change in Small Towns and Rural Areas.* Planner's Press, 2001.

Cheever, John. "A Miscellany of Characters That Will Not Appear." *The Stories of John Cheever.* Knopf, 1978.

Kostof, Spiro. *A History of Architecture: Settings and Rituals.* Oxford University Press, 1995.

Riesman, David. *Abundance for What? and Other Essays.* Anchor Books, 1965.

Scully, Daniel V., "Down Shiftin' for the Self-Service House." Unpublished article, 1975.

——. "Morning Thunder on Highway 101: An Emblematic Tale About Architecture." *Global Architecture Houses* 29 (1990).

Slater, Philip. *The Pursuit of Loneliness.* Beacon Press, 1970.

Venturi, Robert et al. *Learning from Las Vegas.* MIT Press, 1972.

The Bottom of the Lake

Andersen, Bjorn G. *The Ice Age World.* Oxford University Press, 1994.

Pielou, E. C. *After the Ice Age.* University of Chicago Press, 1991.

Sherman, Thomas Fairchild. *A Place on the Glacial Till.* Oxford University Press, 1997.

Wessels, Tom. *The Granite Landscape.* Norton, 2001.

The Otter Mates for Life

Kulish, John. *Bobcats Before Breakfast.* Stackpole Books, 1969.

Boom

Butterfield, Fox. "New England's Siren Call of 80s Becomes Echo of the Depression." *New York Times,* Dec. 15, 1991.

Carlson, Eugene. "New England's Big Recovery: The 'Most Spectacular' Event?" *Wall Street Journal,* Dec. 18, 1984.

Case, Karl E., and Leah Cook. "The Distributional Effects of Housing Price Booms: Winners and Losers in Boston, 1980-88." *New England Economic Review.* May-June 1989.

Dawson, Steven L. "New Hampshire's Parched Economy." *Spectator,* February 1991.

Irwin, David. "Why Nashua, N.H., Came Out No. 1." *Keene (N.H.) Sentinel,.* July 29, 1997.

Mayeroff, Gene I. "Businesses Find New Hampshire to their Liking." *New York Times,* March 23, 1986.

Money. "The Best Places to Live in America." July 1997.

Asphalt, Mon Amour

Adams, Henry. *History of the United States of America During the Administrations of Thomas Jefferson.* 1889. Reprint, Library of America, 1986.

American Road and Transportation Builders Association Web site, http://www.artba.org.

Asphalt Contractor Magazine. "From Liquid Lake Asphalt to Superpave: The Evolution of Hot Mix Asphalt." February 1999.

Asphalt Education Partnership Web site, http://www.beyondroads .com.

Asphalt Institute Web site, http://www.asphaltinstitute.org.

Bayon, Richard. "Trading Futures in Dirty Air: Here's a Market-Based Way to Fight Global Warming." *Washington Post,* August 5, 2001.

Car Busters Web site, http://www.carbusters.org.

Caro, Robert. *The Power Broker.* Random House, 1975.

Center for Public Integrity Web site, http://www.publicintegrity.org.

Colborn, Theo, and Dianne Dumanoski, et al. *Our Stolen Future.* Dutton, 1996.

Communities by Choice Web site, http://www.communitiesbychoice .org.

Emissions Trading Initiative Web site, http://www.etei.org.

Environmental Working Group Web site, http://www.ewg.org.

EPA. "2000 Acid Rain Allowance Auction." March 29, 2000.

———. "EPA Expands Open-Market Trading of Acid Rain Credits." March 20, 1995.

Fagin, Dan, and Marianne Lavelle et al. *Toxic Deception.* Monroe, Maine: Common Courage Press, 1999.

Freeze, R. Allan. *The Environmental Pendulum*. University of California Press, 2000.

The Global Hub for Carbon Commerce Web site, http://www.co2e .com.

Goodman, Robert. *After the Planners*. Simon & Schuster, 1971.

Harte, John, et al. *Toxics A to Z*. University of California Press, 1991.

Hertsgaard, Mark. *Earth Odyssey*. Broadway Books, 1998.

Hofrichter, Richard. *Reclaiming the Environmental Debate: The Politics of Health In a Toxic Culture*. MIT Press, 2000.

Holland, Laurence B., ed. *Who Designs America?* Doubleday, 1966.

Jellico, G. A. *Motopia*. Praeger, 1961.

Kay, Jane Holtz. *Asphalt Nation*. Crown, 1997.

Kearney, Paul W. *I Drive the Turnpikes . . . and Survive*. Ballantine Books, 1956.

Krueckeberg, Donald A., ed. *Introduction to Planning History in the United States*. Center for Urban Policy Research, Rutgers University, 1983.

Lappe, Marc. *Chemical Deception*. Sierra Club Books, 1991.

Leavitt, Helen. *Superhighway — Superhoax*. Doubleday, 1970.

Lewis, David L., ed. "The Automobile and American Culture." *Michigan Quarterly Review,* Fall 1980-Winter 1981.

Lewis, Tom. *Divided Highways*. Viking Penguin, 1997.

Mansfield, Howard. *Cosmopolis: Yesterday's Cities of the Future*. Center for Urban Policy Research, Rutgers University, 1990.

——. "The State of the Lots: Into Each Project a Parking Lot Must Fall." *Metropolis*. April 1985.

McShane, Clay. *Down the Asphalt Path: The Automobile and the American City*. Columbia University Press, 1994.

Meadows, Donella H. "In the U.S., Chemicals Are Presumed Innocent until Proven Guilty." *Keene (N.H.) Sentinel,* December, 17, 2000.

Meikle, Jeffrey I. *American Plastic: A Cultural History*. Rutgers University Press, 1995.

Mowbray, A. Q. *Road to Ruin*. Lippincott, 1969.

National Asphalt Pavement Association Web site, http://www .hotmix.org.

National Cancer Institute Web site, http://www.nci.nih.gov.

National Library of Medicine Web site, http://toxnet.nlm.nih.gov.

New York Times. "Wilson Blames Speeders." February 28, 1906.

Owen, Wilfred. *Cities in the Motor Age*. Viking, 1959.

Scorecard.org Web site, http://www.scorecard.org.

Sustainable Energy Institute Web site, http://www.s-e-i.org.

Steingraber, Sandra. "Living Downstream." *Orion,* Summer 1997.

Tillson, George William. *Street Pavements and Paving Materials: A Manual of City Pavements.* Wiley, 1912.

Wharton, Edith. *A Motor-Flight Through France.* Scribner's, 1908.

Yergin, Daniel. *The Prize: The Epic Quest for Oil, Money & Power.* Simon & Schuster, 1991.

Welcome to the Blueblood Milltown

"The Back-yard." *Century,* July 1898.

Bass, Robert P. "Progressive New Hampshire." *Granite Monthly,* December 1923.

Bicentennial of Peterborough, New Hampshire, October 21, 1939. Peterborough, N.H., 1939.

Carley, Rachel et al. *The MacDowell Colony: A History of its Architecture and Development.* McDowell Colony, 1981.

Carmer, Carl. "Marian MacDowell: Woman with a Possible Dream." *Yankee,* April 1972.

Cooper, Susan Fenimore. "Village Improvement Societies." *Putnam's Monthly,* September 1869.

Cram, Ralph Adams. "The Philosophy of the Gothic Restoration." 1913. Reprinted in Roth, Leland M., ed. *America Builds: Source Documents in American Architecture and Planning.* Harper & Row, 1983.

De Mille, Agnes. *Martha: The Life and Work of Martha Graham.* Random House, 1991.

"Editor's Easy Chair." *Harper's,* October 1882.

"Editor's Table." *New England Magazine,* May 1894.

Egleston, N.H. "Village Improvement." *Century,* March 1887.

Farwell, Parr[is Thaxter]. *Village Improvement.* Sturgis & Walton, 1913.

Fohlin, Paul. "The Empress of Peterborough: Mary Ward Lyon Cheney Schofield." Lecture, 1990. Amended 1999.

Franke, David, and Holly Franke. *Safe Places for the 80s.* Dial Press, 1984.

Graham, Martha. *Blood Memory.* Doubleday, 1991.

Harrison, Gilbert A. *The Enthusiast.* Ticknor & Fields, 1983.

Hart, Rollin Lynde. "A New England Hill Town." *Atlantic Monthly,* May 1899.

"Is Thornton There?" *Peterborough Transcript,* October 17, 1985.

Kessler, Ronald. *The Sins of the Father: Joseph P. Kennedy and the Dynasty He Founded.* Warner, 1996.

Lloyd, Margaret. *The Borzoi Book of Modern Dance.* Knopf, 1949.

Lord, John M. *Mariarden: A Commemorative Tribute to What May Have Been the First Outdoor Theatre in America.* Peterborough, N.H., 1990.

———. "Address at the Peterborough Library, 1991." Mariarden Collection, Peterborough Historical Society.

Mansfield, Howard. *Airline to the Gold Rush.* Unpublished manuscript, 2002.

———. "MacDowell's Artistic Gift." *Washington Post,* August 22, 1988.

Morgan, William. "Peterborough, New Hampshire." *Places: A Quarterly Journal of Environmental Design,* no. 4, 1986.

Morison, George Abbott, and Etta M. Smith. *History of Peterborough, New Hampshire.* Richard R. Smith, 1954.

Muccigrosso, Robert. *American Gothic: The Mind and Art of Ralph Adams Cram.* University Press of America, 1979.

Oliver, Richard. "Cram and Goodhue," in *Master Builders,* edited by Diane Maddex, Preservation Press, 1985.

Peterborough Historical Society et al. *Historical Sketches of Peterborough.* 1938.

———. *A Walking Tour of Peterborough New Hampshire.* 1998.

Peterborough Historical Society Archives: Albert W. Noone: Inventory of Estate, c.1933; Small Collection; All Saints Parish Collection; Bass Family Collection; B. F. W. Russell Small Collection; Cheney-Schofield Collection; Joseph Noone's Sons Co. Small Collection; Mariarden Collection; Old Phoenix Mill Associates Collection; Out-Door Players and Norfleet Camp Small Collection; Peterborough Chamber of Commerce Collection; Peterborough Elders 1930. Small Collection; Town of Peterborough Collection: Town House Clippings and Articles.

Peterborough New Hampshire. A Good Town to Live In. Peterborough, N.H., 1926.

"Peterborough's New Town House." *Peterborough Transcript,* March 7, 1918.

"Portfolio: Current Architecture." *Architectural Record,* October 1924.

Proceedings at the Sesqui-centennial Celebration Held at Peterborough, N.H., October 1889. Peterborough Transcript Office, 1890.

Randall, Peter E. *Our Changing Town: Peterborough 1939-1989.* Peterborough Historical Society, 1996.

Rifkind, Carole. *Main Street: The Face of Urban America.* Harper & Row, 1977.

Robbins, Mary Caroline. "The Art of Public Improvement." *Atlantic Monthly,* December 1896.

———. "Village Improvement Societies." *Atlantic Monthly,* February 1897.

Robinson, Charles Mulford. *The Improvement of Towns and Cities.* Putnam, 1901.

———. *Modern Civic Art.* Putnam, 1903.

Roper, Scott C. *The Role of Elite Perceptions in the Transformation of Landscape in Peterborough, New Hampshire, 1907-1933.* Ph.D dissertation, University of Kansas, 1997.

———. "'The World Is Moving to a Higher Level': The Cost of Progress in Downtown Peterborough, 1913-1921." *Historical New Hampshire,* Spring/Summer 2001.

St. Denis, Ruth. *An Unfinished Life.* Harper, 1939.

Salisbury, Jesse. "Farmerettes Were Trained on the Schofield Estate." *Monadnock (N.H.) Ledger.* February 15, 1990.

Shand-Tucci, Douglass. *Boston Bohemia 1881-1900,* vol. 1, *Ralph Adams Cram: Life and Architecture.* University of Massachusetts Press, 1995.

Shawn, Ted, and Gray Poole. *One Thousand and One Night Stands.* Doubleday, 1960.

Shelton, Suzanne. *Divine Dancer: A Biography of Ruth St. Denis.* Doubleday, 1981.

Sherman, Jane. *Denishawn: The Enduring Influence.* Twayne Publishers, 1983.

———. *The Drama of Denishawn Dancers.* Wesleyan University Press, 1979.

Smith, Albert. *History of the Town of Peterborough.* Press of George H. Ellis, 1876.

Tauranac, John. *Essential New York: A Guide to the History and Architecture of Manhattan's Important Buildings, Parks, and Bridges.* Holt, Rinehart and Winston, 1979.

Terry, Walter. *Miss Ruth: The "More Living Life" of Ruth St. Denis.* Dodd, Mead & Company, 1969.

"Topics of the Time." *Scribner's Monthly,* May 1876, May 1877.

Widdemer, Margaret. *Golden Friends I Had.* Doubleday, 1964.

Wright, James. *The Progressive Yankees.* University Press of New England, 1987.

Big Changes in Small Places

Gass, William H. "In the Heart of the Heart of the Country." *New American Review* 1, 1967.

Garvin, James L. *A Building History of Northern New England.* University Press of New England, 2001.

Hancock History Committee, eds. *The Second Hundred Years of Hancock, New Hampshire.* Phoenix Publishing, 1979.

Hubka, Thomas C. *Big House, Little House, Back House, Barn.* University Press of New England, 1984.

Jackson, J. B. *Discovering the Vernacular Landscape.* Yale University Press, 1984.

Porte, Joel, ed. *Emerson in His Journals.* Harvard University Press, 1982.

Thomas, Peter A. "FEMA-NH-DR-119. Hazard Mitigation Grant Program, Project #31. Section 106 Review: Peterborough Underground Canal. Phase I . . ." Federal Emergency Management Agency. September 18, 2002.

Acknowledgments

For their interviews, I thank Dick Butler, Lincoln Charles, Tom Codman, Jim Coffey, Jarvis Coffin, Alphonse Depres, John Field, George Foskett, Kevin Gardner, Rita Grace, Mitchell Greenwald, Donald Johnson, Alice Phipps Keach, Elizabeth Humstone, Mike Luciano, Rick Monahon, Jeff Porter, Al Ryder, Daniel V. Scully, Bruce Seifer, Jeff Snow, Charles Sullivan, Hilda Wetherbee, Patryc Wiggins.

For their research help, I thank Bill Copeley, librarian, and David Smolen, special collections librarian, of the New Hampshire Historical Society; Alan Rumrill, executive director of the Historical Society of Cheshire County; and Michelle Stahl, executive director of the Peterborough Historical Society. These are exemplary archives and excellent places to work. I also thank Jill Fish and Sally Purrington Hild.

For reading and commenting on selected chapters, I thank James Garvin, New Hampshire state architectural historian, and Michelle Stahl. For their comments at an early reading of the manuscript, I thank Edie Clark, Mary Garland, Judith and Robert Oksner, and Elizabeth Marshall Thomas.

My thanks to Jeannie Eastman for suggesting that I look at the Nims Diaries. Special thanks to Jim Howard for his photography and trespassing skills.

I thank my editors and publishers, Jack Shoemaker and Trish Hoard, for their vision and optimism. Thanks also to my fine copy-editor, Julie Wrinn.

Once again I owe much to my agent, Christina Ward, and to my wife and editor, Sy Montgomery.